Praise for

Let's Talk About EX, Baby

. . . .

"Great praise for Zeifman's brave book, a provocative testimonial full of hard truths about the tragedies of the Toronto dating scene."

—Andrea Dana Eisen, author of *StarSitter*

"*Let's Talk About Ex, Baby* is a funny, insightful and sometimes scary look into the world of dating old guys in the modern world. Prepare for hilarity and a few truly odd moments and enjoy the search for love!"

—Humble Howard, Humble and Fred Show
and author of *The Slime That Men Do!*

"It begins like a Netflix series does—a wait and see if the characters and stories are worth your time. And suddenly, Eureka! Hooked. I took the ride down Karen's memory lane of colourful dates, mates, relational work-ups and wash-outs, in many a story of derailment, disaster and dumpster fires. Plus the get-back-on-the-horse reboots of a human holding on with both hands, to hope. The 'red-flag' tips are brilliant. And lest anyone think this book is fem-centric, there's pictures too fellas, and in the end it's ultimately a how-to that could leave you horny. Or maybe it's just me."

—Jeff Woods, Records & Rockstars

"*Let's Talk about Ex, Baby* takes you on a mind bending, hilarious journey of the ebbs and flows of relationships and the lack thereof. Author Karen, is the gal you want to throw a glass or thirteen back with while sharing the good, the bad and the fugly about her ex partners. Finally, a book where we can ALL find commonalities about our awful EX's."

— **Dr. Sandra Zichermann, Founder, Creator, Blogger: The MOM Rant**

"Karen's done the bad relationships so we don't have to. (But we'll probably go ahead anyway). Sometimes hilarious, sometimes cringy but always insightful! Wherever you are on the relationship spectrum, this is worth the read."

— **Maie Pauts, Midday Host, boom 97.3 Toronto**

"The best part about banging your head against a rock is how good it feels when you finally stop. That's what I wondered when reading Zeifman's honest, funny and occasionally frightening real-life encyclopedia of dating. Did she ever really just think about stopping? Thankfully the answer is finally yes. A true lesson in what many of us have done and what we have learned from it. A must read."

— **Steve Anthony, Canadian Radio & TV Guy (Former Host of CP24 Breakfast)**

"Although I had the *pleasure* of watching many of Karen's relationships unfold in real-time, reading about them was so much more entertaining. Her cautionary fails were fresh, relatable, and downright hysterical. Oh, and the old man was a horrible tipper!"

— **Marianthi Evans, Actress & Bartender at STK, Yorkville**

Daughter G,

Thank you for always being around Mother K loves you & loves our time

HB | HARLOW BOOKS

always...
Thanks for always supporting me. ♡

Kari ♡

Cautionary fails
of a
self-proclaimed
expert
on bad
relationships

Let's talk about EX 'baby

Karen Zeifman

HB | HARLOW BOOKS

Title: Let's talk about EX, baby. Cautionary fails of a self-proclaimed expert
on bad relationships / Karen Zeifman

For information about special discounts for bulk purchases, please contact
business@harlowbooks.com.

ISBN: 978-1-7782581-0-7 (paperback)
ISBN: 978-1-7782581-1-4 (hardcover)
ISBN: 9781-7782581-2-1 (ebook)

Library and Archives Canada Cataloguing in Publication data is available
upon request.

Interior design by THE COSMIC LION
Cover design by Michel Vrana

10 9 8 7 6 5 4 3 2 1

First Edition: 2022

Printed in the United States of America

www.harlowbooks.com
www.karenzeifman.com

This book is dedicated to my son who I hope never reads it. It's way TMI for a child to process without years of expensive therapy. And to my sister for every buzz kill she convinced me to remove. I love you both.

Contents

Foreword

Reading a collection of stories stacked side by side about the hopeful beginnings and calamitous ends of relationships can be funny. But, as you know, it is often more like driving past a series of highway car wrecks. Sometimes you're the passerby, turning down the radio, slowing to rubberneck the carnage. Other times, you're the one being carted away from the flaming vehicle of yet another breakup.

Trigger warning, you will get a bunch of that in this book, and you'll laugh and cringe along the way. But you're going to get something else which separates it from many others; it also may be a way to reframe some of your own experiences. I'll get to that in a moment.

Full disclosure. I have read most of this book, but not all. I didn't read the part Karen wrote about us.

We met in the mid-nineties at really formative stages of our lives. We were both young and brazenly trying to carve out our space. We met in a bar, I think. I don't remember the first time, but what stays with me was that Karen was all the things. I was instantly captivated by how intelligent, hilarious, creative, beautiful, bold, and fiercely independent she was. You'll get that sense. What might not be as obvious is that Karen was so easy to be around, but—this is crucial— not TOO easy, not easy in that chill—let's just hang out—kind of way. If you were going to be with Karen, then, quite rightly, you had to show up. You had to engage; it had to be something. Open and honest communication. I've never felt like anything we ever talked about was left uncovered. This wasn't about oversharing or trauma dumping. It was about connecting and growing. We were lucky to speak the same language with music, art and ideas. We shared what we learned and learned a lot together. I'm grateful for that.

Hindsight that stretches back for a quarter of a century can sharpen the view. What's really come into focus for me, and is what forms the foundation of the woman you will read about, is that Karen was relentless about finding a good fit. She didn't settle, nor did she give up easily. I should know. We tried to make the dating thing work. A few times over the years. At critical moments in our lives, we were there for each other and were better for it. I was trying to remember how our relationship ended. Then I realized it didn't. It simply changed. It never got messy or weird. It didn't blow up, and nobody blocked each other, granted, these were the pre-cell phone and Instagram days. We just found our fit—friendship. Undoubtedly, some of her exes will read this book and not feel the same. But for me, 25 years later, Karen still has that energy and relentless pursuit, and we're still friends. I didn't need to read the section about us to know that we both feel that our relationship was and is a success.

—*George Stroumboulopoulos*

Let's talk about EX, baby

Introduction

Exposed

. . . .

> *"You own everything that happened to you. Tell your stories. If people wanted you to write warmly about them, they should have behaved better."*
>
> **—ANNE LAMOTT**

"Sure I've been to a rub-and-tug, plenty of times actually," my boyfriend blurted out after his one too many Tito shots, from the bottle I always purchased. Immediately after the words left his mouth, he realized that he wasn't talking to one of his buds, bitches or side hoes. When the verticals on my forehead began to appear, specifically my 11s, his story instantly changed. *Hmmm, so I need 20 more units of Botox* and *a new man*, I secretly thought. But having already been inundated with MasterClass ads for FBI negotiator Chris Voss on my socials, I knew that he was lying. Classic Pinocchio Effect. "So let me get this straight. Everyone got a HAPPY ENDING except for you," I repeated in a condescending tone, so he'd hear how ridiculous he sounded. The lies continued to grow, his nose getting bigger and bigger.

"Did he tell you about Vegas?" another ex-girlfriend of his asked during a conversation we had about six months after he and I broke up. Yes, I admit that I creeped her on Facebook, friend-requested her, and then Instant Messaged her like a psycho during my healing process (doesn't everyone?). I was heartbroken, what can I say . . . I wasn't at my most rational. "You mean the trips he took back when he was married, where every single one of his friends cheated on their wives with escorts or strippers, except for him?" I asked. "Oh, he fucked one of them too," she revealed. "He accidentally admitted it to me one night when he was too drunk to keep track of all his lies." I know I shouldn't have cared at that point; we'd been split up for months. But hearing this information from a former flame made me feel better about our demise, and it helped kickstart my journey towards moving on.

So can I NOW step on stage (where's Lil Wayne to escort me?) and accept my award for "Worst Judge of Character in a Tumultuous Drama Series?" I'm the clear winner of this category, and my win is long overdue. My acceptance speech is already written, and ready to go. In fact, you're reading it right now! Or you will be as you turn these pages. Who am I wearing, you ask? Just the same non-designer sweats I've been rockin' daily since the COVID lockdown started. How do I feel being nominated? Grateful to have been selected alongside all of you, and anyone else who has spent years repeating the same patterns of behaviour over and over again, expecting different results. Being a contender in this prestigious category means I, along with all my fellow nominees, can acknowledge our past mistakes and make better choices in the future.

When I reflect on most of my past relationships, I realize that things weren't always as great as they appeared to be on social media or in my head. Once, when I went to the dentist for a routine cleaning, I nonchalantly asked for some laughing gas. No, this wasn't a lame excuse just to take drugs (okay, maybe it was), but they were totally fine with it and hooked me up right away. After my nitrous oxide cleaning and exam was done, I loudly shouted "WHERE'S MY FREE FUCKING TOOTHBRUSH," before realizing that I was already holding it. I was then immediately asked to park my butt in reception and wait 30 minutes before driving home. My experience with men and relationships has been exactly the same as how I feel after my yearly dental visits with the ever-so-loved N_2O . . . cloudy as FUCK and nowhere close to reality. Plus, once you're safely back at home and that magical high's worn off, you're still left with the same loser you didn't even know you were dating!

But 365 days of self-reflection, on top of the countless trips to my therapist's couch (which have been virtual as of late—thanks COVID), has changed this Bitch and given me the courage to throw it all out there. Perhaps I can even help some lost and pained souls in the process. I know there are lots of you out there who have lived through, or are currently living through, relationships with the wrong person. Today I'm all about making real sacrifices and significant life changes that will have a lasting impact and transform me into a better person, instead of just ignoring the reality of a situation and staying put because it's easy or familiar. Every cringeworthy story I've kept private up until now is a lesson I needed to learn in order to grow, and I have some *Juicy Tales* or, more accurately, some *Cautionary Fails* to spill; can someone please hand me that overflowing cup of tea? Here's hoping my mishaps will prompt you to do the opposite. Learn from my mistakes! So, grab yourself a vodka martini with my signature blue cheese stuffed olives of course, and let me explain exactly how I got here. No more excuses. Just the truth. While there are parts you will read that you'll think I made up, I regret to inform you that I didn't. Everything I've written in this book unfortunately *has* happened. Kill me now. And yes, a lawyer has vetted every chapter prepublication, so we're good. Wait, don't cue the orchestra just yet! I'm not done speaking. Stop the teleprompter. Hold your applause . . . I haven't thanked G-d, or my stylist. My nip hasn't even accidentally slipped out of my hoodie yet (oops, wrong show). I haven't slapped Chris Rock. I need more than 45 seconds. And ~~shit~~ (bleep), I still have so much more to say!

Please see back page for legal
NDA Terms & Conditions.
(All interested applicants will be considered.)

Chapter 1

My Ex Left Me for a Trump Supporter

. . . .

Although I'm not here to shame anyone for their political views (yeah right), I would like to take a motherfucking moment of silence for all the badasses out there scratching their heads, like I currently am, at the choices our exes have made after things ended. Like a serious "what the eff were they thinking" pause. The particular confusion I am now talking about has to do with the woman my ex hooked up with immediately after me. And I'm hella confused. Though knowing him as I do, I guess none of his decisions should come as any real surprise. Did he win by a landslide when I became his girl? Of course he did. But he was in way over his head dating someone like me (#sorrynotsorry), and in fact with almost all the runners-up he's ever pursued. So what does a guy do after a number of failed relationships with women completely out of his league? The obvious choice: He finds someone who wants to make America great again. Which might actually be code for: Someone who is more of a loser than he is. Because an imbalance of power never works, and falling for someone more successful can be emasculating for even the most confident of men. After "dating up" for so long, my ex is now choosing to lower his standards instead. Was the plan to give up his rental, move in with me and then get half my house all along? *Bitch please.* He knew I was too smart for him from that very first night in Yorkville. And somewhere deep down, I suppose I did too, if only in retrospect. At the time, I overlooked his "if I moved into your place, you know it would be half mine in three years" comment. I know, I know . . . how could I have missed this?! But my advice now, after some distance and clarity? Bid farewell to that broke-ass 6 and go find yourself that 10 you've always deserved. He's *schtupping* the right girl now. Or, in his words, "my no-strings-attached, long-term hookup, who I've known for 30 years but never once wanted a real relationship with" person. And although I can't understand his post-breakup choices—they're definitely not the majority vote and highly embarrassing to say the least—I now sort of see where he was coming from. And that's okay! I'll be going halfsies on a mortgage with a more qualified and finer candidate very soon. Winning!

When the Jig Is Up, It's Time to Bounce

When a man who hasn't gotten his shit together since his marriage ended more than a decade ago lands a woman like you, he rolls with it for as long as he can. And he fakes it until he gets caught. Ladies, am I right? Because the narcissist in him wants the world to see that he's worthy of an amazing woman like you. For him, it's all about maintaining appearances, keeping up the charade and hiding how he really feels about himself. Unfortunately, though, just like that old carton of milk in your fridge that you know is bad but still need to taste, relationships like this often come with an expiry date. Were things amazing in those first few months? 100%. But research shows that people are on their best behaviour at the start; typically for up to 10 dates. He's the covert sociopath you didn't see coming, who sweeps you off your feet and makes you believe he's never felt like this before. And although you ain't no kid anymore, you'll fall hard and fast for his little bag of *Trix*. Once you're all in, he'll sabotage the relationship and minimize what the two of you had when it's done, as a defence mechanism, convincing himself that everything happens for a reason when he damn well knows that his actions, his mistakes and his own shortcomings were the real cause for the split. So when did things take such a nasty turn? That's obvious. When I started holding him accountable and calling him out on all the lies and bullshit. It's at this precise moment in the relationship, when you begin to question all the inconsistencies, that this type of guy will call you up, say, "thanks for the good time," and announce that he's dropping out of the race. What comes next for an opponent like this? Well, that's simple. First, he'll suppress his feelings and take a break from serious dating, not wanting to deal with another failed attempt at love. Then he'll scroll through his phone looking for a distraction; someone he can easily recycle from the past, who's maybe damaged and hurting as badly as he is; the ballot entry he should have been advocating for the entire time anyway, and the girl he'll eventually catch feelings for. Because when it comes to dating, finding someone on the same level makes the most sense.

The Politics of Dating Down

Why do men who bring nothing to the podium set their sights so high? It's a question successful women like myself have been wondering for years, and remain baffled by to this day. If you're not paying your share of child support or taxes, you drink heavily, and you're in a perpetual rut, doesn't it make more sense to be with someone who's the same? Go find a Queen of the Couch who will sit beside you all day long on your beat-up old throne while the rest of us work. Because with THAT woman, there are no judgements, no responsibilities, no fights, and never any pressure to become a better man. And there was plenty of trash taking up space in my ex's contact list that fit this bill, like the booty call he's had for years, who he literally described as a black-out drunk when we were together, even offering her up to my best friend Joey at the SMOKE-SHOW BBQ like a disposable piece of meat, saying she was "good to go" when we were outside having a cig. Remember? Of course you do. She's the same class act who was in the bathroom stall with another one of your bros that night, and the first pussy you settled on after your marriage ended. And she's the same girl. . . drum roll please . . . that you're currently fucking now. Natch. So for all you insecure men out there with low self-esteem and zero self-worth, vote Republican instead. In retrospect, our campaign wasn't all that promising, and we were never going full-term anyway. So, stay thirsty my friend, and continue burning those spliffs and rocking those plastic Crocs. You're exactly where you're meant to be. It's unanimous. And my debate on the politics of dating down is now over. You're fired.

Election Update

Was it shady of him to stay in contact with me, keep me in the running, and give me false hope while campaigning for her? Hell yeah. But when I found out about their relationship and got tipsy enough to confront him about it, he lied and said it was just sex. Once his slogan changed, and he fell hard for her and got way too clingy, she dumped his Liberal broke-ass and hasn't spoken to him since. Am I surprised he didn't get her vote in the end? Nah. I guess even white women who support Donald Trump have standards too!

Chapter 2

How I Accidentally Became a Gold Digger for a Year

. . . .

To anyone who really knows me, this chapter is somewhat of a farce. Why, you ask? Because I'm actually the girl who chooses Greek salad and pea soup at United Bakers over pricey steak and frites from Ruth's Chris. Or IMAX and Climax instead of a luxurious night out. Well, at least to some extent, that is. You'd never know this, though, because the 'Gram portrays a false perception of how I live my life, and every picture you "like" is obviously a curated visual narrative that's mostly smoke and mirrors. Plus, the hidden nuances of who I am only appear after you've gotten past the walls and metal armour. And although most women would rather dress up, accept expensive gifts and dine in swanky restaurants, getting an impromptu visit from a guy you're crazy about, bearing a single handpicked rose, is a thousand times better than any Hermès Clic H Bracelet I've ever received. So how did this Sexypringle find herself in a Cinda-fuckin-rella *Entanglement*? Props to Jada Pinkett Smith (not *GI Jane*—too soon?) for keeping me real. Let's explore.

Situationships, Are Everywhere

Because I've spent most of my adult life trying to prove that I can do things on my own, I've never paid much attention to these types of romantic arrangements. I'm raising a child alone, have independently purchased a house twice and have been gainfully employed as a Digital Content Producer/ Writer for the better part of [insert number that won't date me or reveal my age]. Still, I have friends from my past who've exchanged sex

for money and won't admit it. This girl Sara I once knew pretended that an envelope she'd received with $1,000 from a one-night stand, which I found on her kitchen counter, was a loan—even though she had no intention of ever seeing the guy again. So, when a man I'd gone on one date with recently texted offering me a Gucci purse, I considered whether I should bite or block. And I get it, I'm ridiculously sexy (whaat?)—I see the draw to lavishing expensive gifts upon me. I'm not gonna lie, it was mad tempting. But do premium women actually fall for this? Spoiler alert! Yes, sometimes we do. I didn't end up meeting the guy dangling his goods, because I've got my own money, thank you very much. I'm no Julia Roberts from *Pretty Woman*, and bartering doesn't really turn me on. P.S. The random incentive pic of your yacht, rather than your dick, was much appreciated! Thank you.

What does a guy 20 years your senior do to lock down a second date after you've said you're not interested? Creep your Instagram and offer to take you to BlueBlood Steakhouse nestled in Toronto's landmark Casa Loma. Right? I said yes, of course, but justified it by thinking I'd been upfront and honest about my lack of interest in any kind of serious relationship. The luxury items soon followed. Once on a weekend getaway, he pulled onto the shoulder of the highway to give me a bottle of Tom Ford *Lost Cherry* perfume (my current fave), just 'cause. He also promised to purchase me a pair of $900 designer kicks for my birthday, which was eight months away at the time, as an incentive to delay the inevitable demise of our mismatched union. Smart. But to my surprise, we fell in love along the way and eventually celebrated our first-year anniversary together. So I have to admit that the bribes worked. But would the relationship have gotten to the next level sans the moolah and all the gifts? Probably not. And this is what I struggle with when I reflect on it. When we started having problems, and he dangled a Louis Vuitton purse in my face to get me to stay, I knew that things were done. So I did what I had to do; I left him, bought the bait myself and never looked back. Thankfully, we didn't end up fighting over custody of Yorkville; he only lives a block away and had paid for every steak dinner, so he probably would have won that one anyway.

When a younger woman enters into a contractual agreement— *ahem,* I mean a relationship—with an older gentleman, the expectations should be carefully laid out, or at least implicitly understood. Both parties should know exactly what to expect. But every once in a while, you'll meet someone who isn't willing to play inside the well-established lines. The rules are there for a reason,

What The Contract Should Look Like

1. You will be wined and dined at some of the city's trendiest spots.

2. Black SUV Ubers will always be pre-ordered and paid for so he can chauffeur you around town in style.

3. Bon Appétit. Only the Crème De La Crème for you. Try to keep your weight in check. (Always say no to the garlic mash, no matter how tempting. It's not worth the Weight Watchers points!)

4. He will engage with the Sommelier to impress you, this is a given, so use this time wisely to brush up on your wine skills.

5. Old men love dessert, mostly Jell-O and rice pudding, but their goal is still the cookie, right? So, he'll probably order one of those too.

6. Share the Top-Shelf Apéritif he'll make a point of asking the waiter to bring by after dinner, then subtly mention how sophisticated he is while seductively sipping it. Senior egos need constant stroking to make up for all their insecurities.

7. When he mentions that he hired *The Geek Squad* from Best Buy to set up his Facebook and Instagram accounts, don't laugh or say your parents do the exact same thing whenever they can't get into Hotmail. He's old. Accept it.

8. Remember he's working overtime to grab a piece of that ass. Hence all the money and time he's spending.

9. *You gon' sip Bacardi like it's your birthday!* He may be playing it cool on the outside, flashing his wealth in your face, but secretly he's humble and grateful for the opportunity to date you.

10. Your 15 minutes of FAME begin now. He will treat you like a celeb!

11. You will receive a ton of expensive gifts. Act surprised as if you were never expecting any of them. This will help with the whole Gold Digger stigma.

Signature: _____   Date : _____

Signature: _____   Date : _____

I Understood The Assignment. Why Didn't He?

Did my ex go rogue when it came to honouring the rules of our unspoken arrangement? Yes. But in the end, I still went along with his unorthodox approach. On one particular night early on in the situationship, while sipping vodka martinis without my beloved blue cheese stuffed olives (the bartender was too lazy to stuff 'em), he reached into his custom Harry Rosen sports jacket to grab his Dollarama bifocals and what appeared to be a printed document. "We're now going to discuss the story of Hanukkah," he insisted, as everyone around us began to eavesdrop. *Are you fucking kidding me?* I remember thinking. I immediately grabbed my phone to make a secret bathroom booty-call to my backup guy and peace out. Just as I was about to excuse myself and escape the monologue that was to follow, he reached under my stool and presented me with a Burberry box, reminding me that I would have to wait until he was finished reading whatever he'd Googled before I could open it.

Was the $600 scarf worth enduring his incredibly boring lecture about a religious holiday (think Christmas, but for Jews)? *At least he wasn't expecting sex,* I thought. I guess making me work for my gift (and of course my meal) was the price I had to pay. He ultimately got what he wanted, because I ended up falling for him eventually, allowing our relationship to burn longer than those eight candles ever did. Perhaps I stuck around to see what else was in store, or better yet, what was coming out of it. I guess we'll never know.

Time Is the Best Present We Can Ever Receive

What lessons did I learn from my days as an accidental gold digger? Well: (1) When it comes to true love, money and gifts hold no real value. Although something that falls within the happy medium between being spoiled rotten and receiving a small token on our birthday would certainly be nice. (2) I'm really not that girl. (3) What you see on social media is only 10% true. Only a fool believes otherwise. Because it's the hangouts, the laughter and the countless hours spent joking about which song to choose for your first dance as husband and wife, those matching finger tattoos you always wanted, or taking his last name (which could be atrocious) that's always mattered most. So on my next interview, I mean date, I'll be sure to focus on what's really important and ask all the right questions. Are you super outdoorsy like I am? Meaning, will you sit under an umbrella in the shade with me on a patio in Yorkville? And (4) Can you offer me your time for free.

Chapter 3

My Boyfriend Ziggy Marley'ed Me

. . . .

> *"The biggest coward is a man who awakens a woman's love with no intention of loving her."*
>
> **—BOB MARLEY**

Once when I was on the phone with my mom while picking up some meat and other Jewish delicacies at Nortown Foods, she overheard me giving the cashier a phone number she didn't recognize. "Who are you giving your reward points to?" she asked. But I should have kept my mouth shut, because the minute I revealed who it was, she went all Nicki Minaj on my ass. "Karen, he broke up with you three months ago. What are you doing?!" Um, what can I say, old habits die hard. Clearly, remaining loyal to a guy who threw an adorable picture keyring of us in his junk drawer immediately after receiving it, wasn't doing me any good. Sadly, this wasn't the only cruel or inconsiderate thing he had done during the course of our relationship. Kindness certainly wasn't his strong suit (he doesn't even own one, no joke). Nor was honesty. He'd been misleading me from the start, professing his undying love and devotion to this unsuspecting gal, without any intention of ever seeing things through. So, with no more free steak coming his way from my accumulating spend (thanks Ma for setting me straight), my deli points and, more importantly, my time are not being wasted on the disingenuous anymore.

Backstage Confessions of an Intoxicated Fan

Some of my best primetime moments with this man were the hangouts early on, during the honeymoon phase, getting tipsy in the private venue I like to call his rental apartment, sipping on two shaken not stirred martinis, while he polished off the remaining bottom-shelf vodka he always kept in his freezer, knocking back Heinekens in between. Gotta stay consistent, right? But these were the bonding moments I should have paid closer attention to: the times he'd either be performing a drunken version of the truth or staging a very elaborate deception. On one particular night of debauchery, he mentioned a life-altering conversation he'd once had with Ziggy Marley backstage at a concert; something he claimed never to have told another girlfriend before. As the story goes, the two of them discussed Ziggy's late father Bob's famous quote, "The biggest coward is a man who awakens a woman's love with no intention of loving her." He then went on to declare to me, with tears in his eyes, that he never wanted this to happen again, admitting that he may have inadvertently misled some women in the past. This was also the same night he chose to say I love "ya" to me for the very first time. Well played [insert name here], well played. *I'm going to be his wifey*, I thought. Looking back, though, everything he presented was an over-the-top production, full of false hope; some cruel truth masked as honest vulnerability. And unbeknownst to me, his signature "I need to work on myself" finale, which I'd later find out was just an encore presentation, would be coming soon. So, were lying, manipulation, and conning his jam? Not sure. I thought I was his greatest hit. It turns out, I was just the headlining act, amongst a future lineup and/or coming attractions about to be played. Or as I like to call it—*ZIGGY MARLEY'ED.*

Throw Him Under the (Tour) Bus. Everyone Else Is!

Here's my advice: Rather than getting together to discuss why things ended (who the fuck cares anymore; it's just code for post-breakup sex anyway), and rather than replying to one of the random texts he sends you to boost his precious ego, reach out instead to the people who know him best, or to an old groupie from a previous tour, or to a friend he's known for 20+ years who thinks you're smokin' hot. Because THESE

are the conversations you need to have in order to move forward, and THESE are the behind-the-curtain stories you want to hear.

> NOV 11, 2020, 4:54 PM
>
> Hi Karen! I remember you from high school. I'm thrilled you reached out.
> When I heard you were with ███, I wanted to call you and tell you don't do it. But....
> Anyways - happy to chat over the phone about what happened. Pass along your number.
> Just know it's not YOU!! He has some major issues.

After spiraling down an online rabbit hole and then speaking with an ex-girlfriend of his on Facebook Messenger, and then later over the phone, I learned that he used the exact same "I need to get my shit together" line on both of us when he ended the relationships. With her, though, he waited three years to do it, wasting so much of her time.

From the same cheesy YouTube videos he sent us (Freddie Jackson's *You Are My Lady*. Really?), to the same secrets he blurted out when he was too intoxicated to keep track of all the deceit, to the same countless breadcrumbs he threw after things ended, or how he would pose for pics, always disingenuously kissing us on the cheek—everything was identical. Literally everything! Even his

"I've never once gotten back together with an ex" proclamation, followed by taking us both back and then changing his mind and calling it quits months later, and his famous "I like to get ahead of myself" mantra (his go-to

> He was an asshole - to you and I both. It's so shitty. They crazy part is that we fell for him, yet he doesn't have much to offer. It's fucked up.
>
> i know...but i will always make fun of you for staying longer LOL...are we there yet? can i make fun of you? hahah
>
> Of course you can!!

excuse every time he'd made a promise or commitment he couldn't keep) . . . it was all verbatim.

What, No Apology Tour?

So where was this "class" act I was supposed to meet at STK Steakhouse on our first date, anyway? Exactly where his ex-wife left him

> I'm so very sorry. He hasn't ever paid child support. ▨▨▨ knows his ex wife husband/bf

over a decade ago, that's where. In *Nowheresville*, to be exact. Or perhaps *Deadbeat Dad Land*. And with all the negative press I received (shoutout to all those who reached out!), I now know that our relationship never stood a chance. Do I believe he went out of his way to intentionally interrupt my life, and inadvertently *ZIGGY MARLEY* me in the process? No. But I should have paid closer attention to his relationship history, because a man who isn't emotionally equipped or capable of real intimacy will always end things first. My bullshit radar should have detected this, but I was too starstruck to notice. I only have myself to blame for hanging onto a broken record for longer than I should have, hoping to fix it, without any success. But holding auditions doesn't guarantee they're ever going to get signed, so don't get caught up in the hype. And by the looks of things, he's been playing this same damn tune on high rotation his whole life, continuously pressing repeat. So, if I'm ever given the opportunity for a meet-and-greet with his next unsuspecting fan who he'll inevitably *ZIGGY MARLEY*, that's one shit-show I'll definitely be attending. Lovey, you've been warned.

ZIGGY MARLEY'ED:

When a guy you're dating, or an actual boyfriend,
falsely commits with NO intention of ever
following through with the relationship.

Chapter 4

Will Ashton Kutcher Be Jumping Out of a Cake Too?

. . . .

When I celebrated my [insert *fake* age] birthday this past spring, I thought things were great. I had just gotten back together with my ex, or so I thought, after an abrupt and confusing exit, and things seemed to be looking up for us. And although we both said we were committed to giving things another try, it turns out I was just his COVID booty call. Yes, this is an actual thing! The minute the city started lifting some of its restrictions, it was buh-bye to this Sexypringle. Let me explain how it all went down. At the time we decided to give things another go, Coronavirus restrictions were still in place, the birthday Zoom link had already been sent out to all my friends, and he had promised to cook me a special dinner just as I had done for his birthday a few weeks earlier. In retrospect, I'm guessing he'd already made the decision to break up with me but needed to at least hold out until after my big day. FYI, wrong choice! No girl ever wants to get *Punk'd* like this. My suggestion to close the night wearing nothing but our *Birthday Suits*, while drinking copious amounts of vodka, was obviously well received—it's an alcoholic's dream date. Know your audience, right? So, what could go wrong? Well about a week prior to our little soirée, he started saying that he might have to cancel, explaining that he hadn't seen his kids in over eight weeks due to the lockdown. I completely understood. Like 100% got it. But I was disappointed and a bit confused—because the minute he finally got the opportunity to spend time with them, he bailed to go to a friend's cottage instead. "What's a few more days?" he justified. "It's already been this long." It was at this precise moment that I knew his needs were always going to come first, regardless of the situation, annual holiday or not. Our night did go ahead as planned, though; presumably because his kids chose to stay at their mom's instead, or because online poker was scrapped. Happy Mutha-fuckin' Birthday to me!

Events Leading Up to Getting Punk'd

There's nothing worse than spending time with someone who isn't quite sure they want to be there anymore. And looking back, there were so many warning signs. Like the night we broke his bed during sex. Yes, I'm that fucking good! But the very first thing he said while we were trying to fix the frame with an Ikea Allen wrench and a magnet was, "you might have to go home tonight if we can't figure this out." Honestly, I didn't understand why he was so opposed to just laying the mattress on the floor and continuing to hang, as I suggested. If their first instinct is to get rid of you, why stay? And if you're about to get *Punk'd* like all those celebs did on Ashton Kutcher's hidden-camera TV show, on your very own birthday, shouldn't he just break up with you first and avoid the "joke"?

Will There Be Cake?

That gourmet meal he promised to purchase, prepare and cook for me? The same one I imagined him slaving over in his tiny galley kitchen? Well, it consisted of two measly beef bones on a Value Village plate. No garlic mash, no mushrooms bordelaise, no mac and cheese with bacon, no duck fat fries, no buttered asparagus, nor a medley of veggies. Nothing. Not even a garden salad for fuck's sake! And all that jumbo cocktail shrimp he had boasted about serving, or any other appetizer for that matter, was nowhere in sight. Where were all the hidden cameras, because this had to be staged. The only thing that actually left the kitchen that night were four over-cooked ribs sprinkled with a dash of Montreal steak spice. I quickly documented the entire absurdity with a photo, in case MTV missed the shot. Pass the HP sauce?

With no trail of rose petals or balloons leading me to an unwrapped gift, a Mariah Carey CD, or a last-minute Amazon purchase, nothing, I soon realized that he hadn't actually gotten me anything. Nada. No presents. No flowers. No candy. No *Dick in a Box*. But who's really shopping online during COVID anyway? The dipping sauces that I asked him to get, after suggesting we play pin the tail on the *Johnson* (blindfold optional)? Well, THOSE he ran around the city looking for, making sure to

collect them all, carefully lining them up on his grandmother's hand-me-down dining table so they were ready to go!

Did he know that making a wish and blowing out a candle was extremely important to me, and that I was highly superstitious about making sure it happened? Yes. I had only mentioned it more times than I had candles. *Geez! Shoutout to my real age.* But the cake never left the fridge. He did, however, promise to drop it off a few days later while on his way to a backyard pool darty* he didn't invite me to. Best boyfriend ever, right? Unfortunately, what I received that afternoon, aside from the shirtless selfie pic complete with a lit cig hanging from his mouth, wasn't sugar-coated. Nor was it a prank. Instead, he delivered the news that we were over, or better yet, cancelled, on his drive back home later that same evening. Oh, and if you're wondering what ever happened to that heavenly slice of chocolate cake he promised me? He prematurely tossed that in the garbage too.

A Sneak Peek Behind the Scenes & Some Deleted Footage

Here's a tip for all you men out there thinking you're doing us a favour by staying with us over an important holiday: Just. Don't. Our big girl pants are on, ready and waiting. We are well prepared to take on any rejection that's coming our way, or anything else below the (Gucci) belt you're planning. Because we've been dealing with pranksters like you our whole damn lives. And that's no joke! Did I know the minute I read his "THANKS FOR BEING YOU" birthday

----

* Darty: A daytime drunken party when the sun's still out.

card (minus any gifts) that things were over? Plot twist: I'm no fool; of course I knew. And to think I still had to spend an entire evening with him after receiving this blow. P.S. including "you are sooo YUMMY" definitely added some extra entertainment value, but didn't increase your ratings. Just saying.

We Interrupt this Regularly Scheduled Relationship . . .

Our romantic Valentine's Day celebration back in February 2020 had been a completely different scene than the disastrous birthday celebration that would follow only a few short months later. From the two dozen long stem pink roses he handed me (he'd never waste his money paying for delivery), to the medium-rare steak he prepared with, wait for it, a side Caesar salad and a gourmet dessert, to his thoughtful words and the way he treated me the entire evening; it was all the complete opposite of the excruciating past birthday I later endured. The stark contrast between the two events made me question why he changed the channel in the first place? I thought the next 10 seasons had already been renewed.

Even his post to my Facebook page "Happy Valentine's Day to my Sexy Pringle . . . U r the YUMMIEST!!! Love you!!!" had been a huge gesture on his part. He hardly ever used social media, and when he did, it almost never included anything from his personal life. He was sending out mad "serious" co-star vibes, to me and to the world. This beautiful declaration of his devotion had also been accompanied by an adorable picture of him affectionately kissing me (his signature pose), viewed by 1,000+ of my *closest* friends, along with a romantic card attached to my long stem roses. Fast-forward to my birthday, which included very little of anything except for a

Zoom party that he chose to remain off-camera for. In retrospect, Valentine's Day was so incredibly different from my birthday that it's almost laughable now (following a good cry). So why punk someone on their birthday and then end things a few days later? This I will never understand. What I do know is this: Going through the motions never works. Because our intuition kicks in the minute they start acting differently or pen us an ironic loveless note. Message received. Next time, just humour us and make sure to leave before the season ends, or at least prior to when the shit-show is scheduled to tape. There are so many other D-listers we can party with on any given occasion. It didn't have to be you. And thanks again to Ashton Kutcher and MTV for opting not to air this lost and final 2020 reboot episode of *Punk'd*.

His Birthday Celebration

For his birthday a few weeks prior to mine, I made sure to lay out a charcuterie board, with an array of gourmet meats and cheeses I carefully selected (Ramsey-approved!) along with a multitude of very thoughtful and romantic gifts. This is in sharp (cheddar) contrast to the mini Pringle cans and leftover pizza dips he would later throw on the table for my birthday. But this is not a tit for tat. Instead, I'll take the low road and describe how completely different our celebrations actually were, and how each one clearly corresponded to our respective headspace at the time. His over-the-top bash for two wasn't anywhere close to the disaster I was forced to endure. But I didn't have any hidden agenda (or hidden cameras) during my planning of his special day, as he obviously had with mine. I certainly worked overtime, or maybe a bit extra, because we had just gotten back together. Did I shamelessly wear an apron I'd ordered from Amazon (a COVID purchase) over my naked body while cooking his fancy dinner? Damn right I did. You're welcome, birthday boy. His fancy dinner included a considerable amount more than the raw meat he threw in the oven for me. Bonus points for trying, right?

In retrospect, getting him such a sentimental and highly personal gift so soon after our reconciliation was probably a bit premature. Okay, definitely premature. My bad. But remember, I had no idea he was already planning his second split. I was all in, thinking of all the future fun we'd be having soon. I'd chosen 10 adorable (FaceTuned, of course) pics of us from happier times and ordered him a custom vintage *View-Master* like the one we all had as kids. His meh reaction to it said it all. Thank goodness the Google Chromecast and the six other gifts were a hit though! Whether he liked them or not, at least I tried. And that's the point. But when it was my turn to be celebrated, he simply couldn't be bothered. And it was this lack of effort or planning that hurt the most, although the bar he had set following our pointless reunion (not to be mistaken with his liquor cupboard) was already pretty damn low to begin with.

Did I keep my mouth shut when he proudly read me the birthday card his grown daughter had given him? You better believe it! But her message was loud and clear, or at least it was to me. And as he welled up with tears while reciting her encouraging words, I couldn't help but feel uncomfortable. It basically said, in not so many words, *I know you're a loser daddy, but I still love you anyway*. And the poor guy was clueless. When your own kid is offering you up a pep talk, encouraging you and telling you that things will hopefully turn around, that ain't good. But I'd been doing the exact same thing: Enabling him and being a supportive, loving and loyal girlfriend when I knew deep down that he was a dud. Except in my case, there weren't any ties by blood or marriage keeping us together, so I always had a choice whether to be in the relationship or walk away.

#CANCELLED

Was his very first COVID birthday, unlike mine, a huge success? Yes. Of course it was! Because I'd taken care of every last detail, which, correct me if I'm wrong, is what you're supposed to do when you're in a relationship and care about the person you're with. Was I right there beside him, er, on top of him, for his birthday Zoom? It wasn't a secret that we were back together at this point, so it never occurred to me to be anything but right there next to him both figuratively and literally. During my virtual party, he remained hidden in the kitchen scrubbing a dirty meat pan with an S.O.S pad. I also made sure to bring out his cake after we forgot about it the night before, so he could blow out his candles, make a wish and avoid the year of bad luck he'd eventually curse me with. Thankfully, we've both had another trip around the sun since we ultimately parted ways, and all the horrible memories

I've been replaying in my head since have recently been erased and recorded over. I doubt his most recent celebration this past May was as memorable as I made his the year before. Unless he's found someone willing to give him that massage. But his icing on the cake left when I did, the morning after.

Chapter 5

Collecting a Wagon Full of Red Flags

. . . .

O nce while I was putting my son to bed and waiting patiently to drop and roll out of his room, a suggested video popped up on my iPhone from talk show host Steve Harvey saying, "don't get into the habit of collecting red flags. Before you know it, you'll have a whole wagon full of them and you'll still be with the same loser." It was at this moment that I began to question my own search history but, more importantly, the mistakes I've repeatedly been making over the years when it comes to choosing men. Had I been ignoring some obvious warning signs? You betcha! British relationship expert and dating coach Mathew Hussey describes this type of selective memory, where women conveniently become forgetful, make excuses for bad behaviour or let things slide as the "One Day Wager," and claims that we trade in our time, energy, emotions and intimacy in hopes that one day these guys will eventually become better men. But this rarely ever happens. So, take it from me, betches; red flags are your cues to leave. Stop investing time in the wrong men! The goal here is to keep your little red wagon empty, right?

(Un)Employed, Or Fake News?

I once had a boyfriend who'd told me over drinks on our first date that he was in commercial real estate. "Perfect," I'd thought, "we can meet at What A Bagel on my WFH days." But we never did share that lox and cream cheese platter. I'm not sure why, since he had more free time than anyone I knew; it turns out he wasn't actually working. Of course, I had no idea at the time—buddy was still trying to get laid, right? When he'd say he was on his way to a client meeting, I believed him. But it was just a cup of Java and a smoke with another jobless Joe at the mall after carpool drop-off. He eventually did come clean, but waited until after we'd fallen in love to tell me. Smart. One night he called me with an "innovative" and "brilliant" idea that he wouldn't shut up about: he was going to buy an expensive tripod and record himself on video for potential employers. "I could just hold your iPad for you," I suggested, "or buy you that $10 Selfie Studio Light clamp I saw on Etsy that does the exact same thing?" But he was looking for a distraction, not a job. And all those wasted hours listening to him go on and on about the customer reviews and 5-star ratings, trying to be supportive? Well, I'm never getting those back. Plus, if he was actually serious about finding work, wouldn't his employment history, or at least a profile pic, be up on LinkedIn? Today, that extravagant and unnecessary $150 three-legged stand he shamelessly charged to his mom's Amazon Prime account sits in his hallway closet collecting dust, having never once been used for its intended purpose.

Red Flag Tip #1

It's not our job to fix 'em, change 'em, parent 'em, raise 'em or carry 'em. You want a partner, not a (pet) project. If he doesn't work, it's never gonna work.

FAT-Shaming

A few years ago I crossed the U.S. border and went on a road trip to Buffalo to see Mariah Carey (my first true love) with my 65-year-old boyfriend. He even exchanged the ticket I'd previously purchased and opted to sit alone so I'd be closer to the stage. Sweet, right?! Honestly, it was the perfect mini-vacay. But the next day on our drive back home, he revealed a side of himself that I'd never seen before. After morning sex (no he didn't take Viagra, as I'm sure you're all assuming) and an extra late checkout, we decided to grab breakfast. At this point I was starving, bordering on hangry, and I wanted to enjoy some carbs with zero guilt. Vacation calories don't count, right? But he had other plans. After driving around for what felt like forever, we settled on a Wendy's drive-thru. He ended up ordering nothing, and I chose nuggets, fries and an extra-large coffee. At the order window, the lady on the muffled speaker asked how many chicken pieces we wanted. "She'll have six," he said, even though I was sitting right beside him. Umm, hello . . . why not ask me? "We've also got a nine pack or a 20–" she continued, but he interrupted her and hastily said, "she doesn't need more than six." He then turned to me and blurted out that I should be watching my weight. Wow. I was mortified. And of course mad AF. I'd never been body-shamed by a partner before, so I grabbed the bag and threw it in the back seat, clearly upset by his comment. And that afternoon treat *he* was hoping to receive—off the side of the road (or while driving)—wasn't happening. Getting Burger-Shamed at Harvey's for ordering too many toppings on my patty by another ex-boyfriend a few years back was nothing in comparison to this! After telling me to "cool my jets"* (um . . . did the 1950s just call?), he back-pedalled and said he was just concerned about my tummy. Whatever his reason was for the comment, I'll never forget how it made me feel. Ironically, after dropping 15 pounds later that same year, he became extremely jealous and worried that I'd leave him for another man. FYI, my Frosty† still brings all the boys to the yard, no matter what my size, so sip on that, old man.

Red Flag Tip #2

If he fat shames you, shame on him. Next time, make a healthier choice!

. . . .

* Cool Your Jets—A term old men (65+) use when they want women to CALM DOWN. Something you should never say to a woman. Ever.

† Frosty—Maybe the best item on Wendy's menu. Is it a milkshake? An ice-cream? No one actually knows. No one actually cares either; it's delicious.

SHIT-Shaming

To all those who snicker or make a fuss when someone takes a massive dump at the office, saying things like "Ew gross," "I wouldn't go in there if I were you," or "It wasn't me, I swear," please stop. Like immediately. It's something we all do and using a public restroom for its actual intended purpose seems like the logical choice. Unless you're like my friend Emily who, back when we both worked at BlackBerry, held her bowels for six hours until she got home, even though most of us occasionally have to *Number 2* when we're outside of the confines of our own address. No one should embarrass or humiliate us for doing something that's completely natural. Right? This brings me to my FAT-Shaming boyfriend, who would also get extremely agitated every time I went potty in his condo. Apparently, his shit didn't stink. But if my faux-pas was so incredibly offensive to him, maybe he should have thought twice about dumping cocaine onto his glass side table every G-ddamn time we were behind closed doors. Oops, maybe I really am a (party) pooper? And it's not like I had a choice; when you gotta go, you gotta go. Plus, that shit's laced with laxatives! Did I enjoy frantically searching for extra rolls of toilet paper or Glade Air Freshener underneath the sink every time I was at his place? Hell no. How many times can I apologize? It was only a few spritzes of your *Old Spice*, you (anal) cliché, okay?

Red Flag Tip #3

If he's getting angry every time you get the urge to go, that's one pile of crap you need to flush. If your man can't handle you going doo-doo, he's a definite don't-don't.

Anger Issues & Adult Temper Tantrums

The turning point with this ex-boyfriend came right after we'd gotten back together for the second (and final) time. Yes, I know—big mistake. Everyone warned me not to go there again, yet I didn't listen. But this particular incident, which happened in the basement laundromat of his apartment building (yes, he still rents; is this too a red flag?), changed everything and I haven't looked at him the same since. When a sweet religious woman frantically came running downstairs with her four young children in tow after forgetting to grab her clothes from the dryer, he came at her full force. "I've been waiting 45 minutes you FUCKING CUNT" he cursed. Yelling "C-U-Next-Tuesday" to a woman over washables is a tad extreme, don't ya think? "How could you call her that in front of her babies?" I asked. "You're a father too." But not taking his side only triggered him more. "Trust me, her kids know she's a cunt; it's not like they haven't heard it before," he shouted back at me. *Um, I'm pretty sure they haven't,* I thought to myself. At this point I couldn't hide my disdain anymore, and my gut was telling me to bolt ASAP. So I threw $5 in rolled coins on the stacked milk crates he was using as a makeshift coffee table, and tried to make a clean break. Unfortunately, I somehow justified the incident and remained in the relationship for another spin, rather than treating it as a serious red flag.

Red Flag Tip #4

If your man uses the C-word, wash his mouth out with *Tide*. More importantly, if he gets banned from the downstairs laundromat, skip the fabric softener and leave that stain once the cycle is done.

Never Having Your Back

Same guy, different story. Isn't it amazing how disappointments can add up with certain dudes? If you don't feel supported and/ or he isn't making any real effort to make you happy, this too is a red flag. In retrospect, there were sooo many *UNGESTURES** that I should have noticed. One time I called him up crying after accidentally deleting every text, voice memo and YouTube song we had ever sent each other. He pretended to care about how upset I was, and I believed him when he said he'd help me get them all back. "Don't worry, Pringle, I've still got everything on my phone, so there's no need to get your panties in a bunch." He already knew about the Keepster app I'd found that turned texts into a hardcover

. . . .

* UNGESTURES—The opposite of a gesture (regardless of how big or small). When a boyfriend doesn't consider your feelings and never does anything nice.

book, which I was secretly planning on gifting him, so it would have been really easy for him to replace all that I had accidentally erased. And although I admit I was being melodramatic, he assured me that I could always come to him no matter what the issue, and he'd take care of it. But surprise, surprise—we never did make it to the Apple store as promised, or call iCloud Support, even though I mentioned it a gazillion times. I'm guessing he was too busy researching over-priced tripods to help a girl out. Ironically, after doing some ex-tremely hurtful things to him shortly after we broke up, like airing all his dirty laundry (*um. . . there weren't any available basement dryers at his place*), he immediately found a way to retrieve everything I originally lost and then turned around and threatened to use it all against me. Okay, maybe I deserved that! But where was all this ef-fort when we were together? "I've got hundreds of pages of conver-sations, Kare, all printed up, highlighted, and ready to go," he said. "How would you like it if I mailed them all to your parents?" Really dude? Unfortunately, his troubleshooting skills, initiative, and what could have been a kind gesture, reared its ugly little head after it was too late.

Red Flag Tip #5

Take note of the *ungestures*, as they're a clear indication of what's (not) to come. If your man doesn't have your back, call your chiroprac-tor instead.

Immaturity, Excuses & Lies

In retrospect, of course I should have paid closer attention to his inconsistencies. Because his words and his actions never once lined up, and everything he said was mostly just what he thought I wanted to hear. But these are the contradictions that let us know exactly what kind of person we're really dealing with. Remember, they're always on their best behaviour at the beginning of the relationship. After only a few months in, it was clear that I was dating a child. One day while hanging out at his place, we heard some loud honking and shouting coming from the street. We immediately went onto the balcony to check it out. What followed is something only *Jackass*'s Johnny Knoxville would do. My 51-year-old boyfriend ran to his fridge and grabbed some raw (non-organic) eggs to throw at the pile-up of cars. Is this the kind of role model I wanted for my son? Definitely not. Or a long-term partner? Looking back now, of course not. Another time, after mentioning that I was going downtown to meet some friends for drinks, he spent most of the day begging me to stop by his place on my drive home so he could romantically run down three flights of stairs and kiss me. Sweet, right? I was "all in." When I texted to say I was only two minutes away, he claimed that his buds were over and that he couldn't come downstairs. WTF? After I sent him a passive-aggressive text indicating clear disappointment and confusion, he immediately called me back promising in a hushed tone to make it up to me the next day. But it didn't add up. He could have been downstairs and right back up in less time than it took to make the pointless call. Take the elevator dude. To this day, my friend Donnie is convinced that he was with another woman. "Kare, I'm a guy," Donnie would tell me. "I don't care how many of my buds are over—if a hot chick calls, I'm going down. End of story. No other explanation makes sense." And although I'll never know the truth about this one, it was probably the first of many lies, and Donnie was probably right.

Red Flag Tip #6

Toss that bad egg out the window (or even off your balcony). If you're questioning everything he says (this early on), the relationship is already cracked and you ain't never putting Humpty back together again.

Zero Communication Skills

If you're trying to build a relationship with someone who doesn't know how to effectively resolve conflict, you're fucked. And this is the most frustrating red flag of all, because it's the easi-

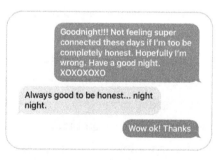

> Goodnight!!! Not feeling super connected these days if I'm too be completely honest. Hopefully I'm wrong. Have a good night. XOXOXOXO

> Always good to be honest... night night.

> Wow ok! Thanks

est one to fix. But if it's always a one-sided conversation that ends with you getting upset, there isn't much to work with. Once after my boyfriend got severely wasted and went on to embarrass me in front of his friends who I was meeting for the first time, I tried talking to him about it later that night. But he shut the conversation down and wasn't interested in resolving it, let alone admitting that he might have a drinking problem. On another night, after getting sloshed yet again, he bragged about banging another chick to a group of men—right in front of me. When I texted him later that same evening to tell him I was so done, rather than try to work things out or apologize, his response back to me was #metoo, in true Harvey Weinstein style. The next day he back-pedalled and pleaded drunken immunity. As time went on, he'd shut off his phone completely whenever there was the slightest hint of tension, sometimes for up to five hours at a time, conditioning me like a Pavlov dog never to raise my concerns. But for effective communication to take place, both parties need to put forth an effort, right? Or at least participate in some healthy and constructive dialogue. The best apology is changed behaviour, but after countless disappointments and the silent treatment, he had already checked out.

Red Flag Tip #7

If he shows zero communication skills, it's time to rate the relationship a zero. When a guy doesn't make the effort, it doesn't mean you try harder. It means you can do better. Move on.

Substance Misuse

I do have addiction issues that also includes YoU! Lol

> I'm the best addiction you've ever had

I'm also too old for you! I don't date 32 year olds ha

Alcoholism and drug abuse are probably the number one red flags to watch out for, since they are the most dangerous. Is it a coincidence that my last two back-to-back relationships were both with men who appeared to be struggling with addiction? Not sure. One is supposedly in recovery right now, working the steps (although every Insta pic I see from the Finsta* account I created shows otherwise), while the other one is in 100% complete denial. But they're no longer my burden anymore; my condolences to the next girls. One night when the 65-year-old and I were attempting to have sex in his car (um yeah, I'm so that girl when my son's awake at home and I'm out of options), he couldn't "get it up," which was completely out of character for him. It turned out, after a ton of prodding, that he'd taken opioids that night and had been abusing them the entire week (and probably longer). "What? Why?" I asked. But a true addict never gives a straight answer. And therein lies the problem with dating unhealthy men. The other failed relationship could have been avoided, if someone, ANYONE, would just have warned me about some of his shortcomings. It was no secret; common knowledge actually, that he had a few problems. Everyone seemed to know except for me. My first clue should have been the two ounces of vodka he needed to begin every night with, even for Netflix and Chill sessions, or when he'd sneak into his kitchen for secret shots every time I was at his place. There's no point in shaming him any further though. He's already lost a marriage, tons of friends throughout the years, other fantastic women, and of course me, because of it. Ultimately, relationships with addicts are complete *K-OS* and never work, 'cause "everyday is Saturday night" and they will always choose their addiction over you. My advice: Don't go there. It's never worth it in the end.

. . . .

* Finsta—The fake Instagram account you create to creep on an ex boyfriend without their knowledge (or consent).

Red Flag Tip #8

Don't date addicts; you'll be saving yourself months, if not years, of heartache and Al-Anon Family meetings.

Disrespects Women

This was the guy who'd literally jump out of his beloved Audi with switched-out black rims every time he picked me up for a date, just so he could open my car door. But his perfect gentleman persona disappeared right around the time he said that "the most exciting part about dating someone new is all that fresh pussy." Classy, right? One night after dinner at a lovely Italian restaurant with another couple, he insisted on going to Drums N Flats, his neighbourhood watering hole, where he considered himself to be Mayor, even though the rest of us were quite happy staying put. But he wanted to get shit-faced at a new location instead, so we left like a group of 20-something bar-crawling college kids and headed to his bar of choice where he was about to debut yet another red flag. After ignoring me for hours, which was a first for him, and comparing

> Wanted to mention that I didn't really love all the stories you were telling groups of people about other girls in front of me / it felt a bit disrespectful

Sorry about that

Obviously I think you're the best

Night night

PRIMETIME GOLD

Today 1:05 PM

I'm sorry that I was an a-hole last night. Will do my best to not let that happen again...

sexcapades with a group of drinkers, including local radio host John Gallagher who was also there that night, while I stood beside him, he decided to go three-for-three when a friend of his came by to introduce herself to me. "When I first met this chick, I grabbed her tits so hard to see if they were real," he vulgarly said after she'd walked away. "But she didn't get mad, and actually let me feel 'em." He added insult to injury with his "don't worry, Kare, your tits are fucking fabulous too" which he loudly exclaimed to the entire group left standing there. Really, Seinfeld? Tell me something I don't already know. But bragging about conquests and objectifying women is so NOT cool. And with me, his girlfriend, standing right beside him?! After mentioning it to him via text, I tossed it into my already overflowing wagon, and we never spoke of it again.

Red Flag Tip #9

If he disrespects you, he's not worth your respect in the first place. Leave the table when love is no longer being served.

Dangles Money & Gifts to Keep You Interested

The old man I dated for over a year, who used his wealth to reel me in, would often send me Bob Barker "come on down" offers to try and change my mind after I'd tell him I just wanted to be friends. His 14-year-old daughter was also a regular contestant, and even received a $150 basic white tee once, after she snatched his phone,

Do you want to meet at Roosters at 3?

I can't I'm leaving early today. Plus I don't think it's a great idea for now.

Do I have to threaten you with my secret weapon (GUCCI) when you have so much contempt for me?

You are Hilarious

Your secret weapon should be kindness and honesty hahahaha

changed his iCloud password, and read every private text message we'd ever sent each other. "She steals from you, and you reward her with a gift from TNT to smooth things over?" I asked him. But for him, money and conflict always went hand in hand. Once, following surgery to remove polyps on my cervix, he didn't offer to take care of me post-op or even come by my place for a visit. After expressing my disappointment, he ordered me a $300 get-well basket as a peace offering instead. A few weeks later after our next fight, he sent me a random pic of a Prada purse, treating me like a complete whore instead of just apologizing for his behaviour. But it didn't stop there. Towards the end of our relationship, after one of our many breakups, he offered to buy me a white leather designer belt, on top of the black one he'd already given me, in exchange for another chance. He even showed me the Gucci order number on his phone as proof once I agreed to meet him. During dinner, though, he didn't hear what he was hoping to. I told him I wasn't for sale, polished off the expensive steak he bought me and immediately ended things, marching into Holt Renfrew the next day to purchase that belt myself.

Red Flag Tip #10

If he dangles gifts in front of you as a get-out-of-jail free card, it's probably time to declare him "guilty-as-charged" and exchange him (even without the receipt) for someone new.

Love Bombing (Surprise, He's a Narcissist)

If he texts you Beyoncé's "Crazy in Love" music video a week after meeting for the first time, as my love-bombing boyfriend did, be-

Ok. Be careful

Of course

LOVEY

Lovey where r u?

Call me back

Pls

I had so much fun with you tonight. We always have such a good time together!!! Im your most fun friend lol

U r definitely FUN!!! 😘

And my person!!!

🩶

ware. You may be dating a narcissist. And the relationship will most likely end as quickly as it began. No Fourth of July fireworks here, because you ain't making it past March. While the extravagant displays of affection (AKA Love Bombs) will commence from date number one, don't be fooled. It's their secret weapon. These actions are strategically placed to gain your love and trust, in the form of flattery, compliments, romance, or promises of a future. Back in December of 2019 when I first met my con, our chemistry was explosive, and he would prematurely talk about "us" every chance he got, bringing up marriage, forever, and gushing that I was his person and his plus-one all within the first month. I fell for every single line. Unfortunately, he was just manipulating me into thinking he'd found his unicorn. So, when a friend recently called to tell me that the Trump supporter (otherwise known as the girl he hooked up with immediately after me) dumped him for using these exact same Love-Bombing tactics, I was a bit taken aback. Not because I wasn't over him, but because he'd taken something special that I thought was strictly between us, and casually applied it elsewhere. Proving once again that what we shared was in fact NOT real, and that "his person" is whoever he randomly happens to be with (apparently he tells every new target this, even booty-calls). A Baskin Robbins featured scoop, a KERNELS POPCORN seasonal flavour, or an employee of the month, honoured briefly on the wall [length will vary depending on girl] until it's time to find a new supply.

Red Flag Tip #11

Don't cling to "mistakes" because you've spent too much time making them. Love-Bombing usually equals the relationship blowing up.

Chapter 6

I Went to Rehab for Weed Addiction, Twice

. . . .

S o, I'm the Sandra Bullock wannabe who, wait for it, went to rehab for weed. Twice. But if smoking marijuana is just as common as contracting HPV now is for millennials, how did a girl like me end up at North York General Hospital (for waaay longer than *28 Days* I might add) in their outpatient Substance Abuse and Addiction Program? Well, back when I was in my twenties, I was lighting up spliffs on the daily. No biggie, right? But I couldn't turn in at night without getting high. I guess you could say I was a functioning addict. And that nice Jewish boy, let's call him Aaron, who I was dating at that time? He took a pass on me, rather than *pon the left-hand side*, for falling into a weed coma at his place one too many times. The end of that relationship still remains one of my biggest regrets to this day. My rock bottom finally hit while perusing new releases at the local Blockbuster Video I frequented every day, not face-down in a gutter at 4:20 as one would assume. When the salesclerk Jenny (of course we were on a first-name basis), who looked to be around my age, asked if I was in a hurry, I said "sure, I can stay and hang." I literally had nothing else going on and was excited to be making a new friend. Plus, my old bestie *Mary Jane* had become a bit of a bore as of late. Turned out, she just wanted me to watch the store while she ran across the street to grab a sub and a bag of Doritos. It was at this precise moment that I knew my life was heading in the direction of my couch, and that something needed to change. Fast.

The Laughing Stock of The Joint

Although people still think it's fucking hilarious that I went to rehab for pot, and I could easily have my own *TED Talk* or more realistically a *Just For Laughs* comedy special on the subject now, I don't want to minimize the importance of what I actually did, even if marijuana isn't considered to be a real drug. Because today it's like getting Botox when you have no wrinkles; it's good to be proactive and take action, with a little assistance, to prevent looking exactly the same as every other 40+ year old will in ten years. But everyone in group therapy still made fun of me for months, accusing me of being a *21 Jump Street* narc or an undercover journalist, like Josie Geller in *Never Been Kissed*. Really? And even though I was secretly enjoying all the unwarranted attention and drama my presence was creating, I had so much to learn. Like maybe not telling them about the shots of codeine cough syrup I'd done the night before, completely polishing off the entire bottle, just for fun. "This is considered a relapse?" I asked. I thought I was just being clever and had found a loophole. But abstinence was their number-one rule. No exceptions. And this

Rainy Day Woman had just broken it. Needless to say, an in-depth discussion of my drinking all that over-the-counter medicine monopolized the entire morning session, and my addiction seemed to be carrying more weight than the 28 grams I rolled in on.

Can I Be Blunt?

I once received a two-page fax (remember those?) at the radio station Z103.5 where I worked as a copywriter, from my friend Sean,* who was concerned about my excessive marijuana use. But everybody was toking, so why the office ambush? The front desk receptionist, Pauline, who received the fax, plus every co-worker in my office, read it before I did. And although I almost got fired that day, it forced me to recognize two significant things; first, that my behaviour was clearly affecting other people, and second, that I needed to find a new friend who used email instead. But if the only real stigma associated with stoners is that we're all lazy AF, then what's the problem? Everyone parties, no? Well for starters, I was moody, withdrawn, completely unmotivated, and not exactly pleasant to be around. When my parents started to take notice, they sent me a Xerox too. Okay, not really. But after a few honest conversations, and a hard look at myself in the mirror, I decided to embrace the semi-circle and get clean. And it wasn't until a few dimes later, in my forties, when a deadbeat boyfriend started exhibiting these same behaviours, that I realized I was right back where I started. Except this time, I was front-row-center for a show I wasn't interested in rewatching.

Was rehab a success? Yes. But it all depends on how you look at it. Because the truth is, I'm not entirely sober. There have been *bumps* along the way: I've partied with *Molly* a few times, and I still go out for martinis with blue cheese stuffed olives. Often. But I haven't smoked a joint since. So regardless of the fact that I still have some minor dependencies, or habits as I like to call them, I don't abuse drugs, or use despite the negative consequences anymore, which is why I entered rehab in the first place. Ironically, I almost ended up with a chronic user and alcoholic, who's unemployed, and incapable of maintaining a healthy relationship because of this. And when I think about how close I came to joining his Scooby *Doobie* ass back on his couch again after I'd worked so hard to get the hell off mine, I appreciate that uncomfortable wobbly plastic hospital chair I sat in three times a week for six hours a day that much more!

It's High Time You Quit

Today I have zero tolerance for potheads. 'Cause let's be real . . . Snoop-Dogg's the only one actually pulling this off. Right? If you ask me, the rest of you dopeheads should just stick to *Gin and Juice*. And I get it—no one's asking. But I can't help it. The PTSD from my horrible experience with weed has taken me to a dark place. A bad trip, so to speak. Full of judgments and opinions I should probably keep to myself. And the stigma people seem to have forgotten about now that it's legal, doesn't suddenly make it more glamorous to me, the way blow was in the '80s, or any less addictive. Ask *Alexa* about weed dependencies if you don't believe me. The only thing that's really changed is how it's purchased. Meaning, we don't have to fuck our dealers or let 'em do bumps off our titties anymore to score a baggie. At the end of the day, it's just a lazy man's drug IMO, with my ex being the poster child. Want to know what happened with that brilliant idea he poached from *FabFitFun* selling monthly subscription boxes for outdoor survival gear? Nothing. Because he was probably stoned out of his fucking mind when he came up with it. Plus, dopeheads aren't exactly known for their follow-through. So, take it from me and learn from my experience: a double-baked potato with all the toppings is definitely something we all want to eat (even if we're avoiding carbs), but a fried loser like you? Is a Puff. Puff. Pass.

. . . .

* This is dedicated to Sean Lockman who left us in 2015. Thanks for all the great memories, laughs and late-night college studio sessions. And for caring enough about me to call me out on my shit, even if your message was delivered via fax!

Chapter 7

Guys Like You
I Won't Date
Anymore

. . . .

My Vision Board inspired by Queen Oprah hangs prominently in my bedroom across from where I sleep and in my line of sight. Displaying a collage of cut-out pictures and affirmations all designed to help me reach my relationship goals, it's the first thing I see when I wake up in the morning. Since the past few years have been met with, let's just say, a few disappointments, I try to release as much positive energy into the universe as I can to manifest my Liam Neeson (did I just reveal my age and possibly some daddy issues?!). But there's something Ms. Winfrey and the famous self-help book, *The Secret*, forgot to mention, and that's to gather all of our "been there, done that . . . bought the fucking tee-shirt" moments and pin those bad boys up too. Totally kidding. Do not do this. It will cancel out every proclamation you cut out of *Glamour* magazine and completely kill the vibe. But visualizing what isn't working in our lives anymore is just as important as any aspirational quote, so we can finally stop repeating our mistakes. I use Post-It Notes to help with these daily reminders, but anything will do, as long as it's something. Because knowing what our deal-breakers are, and everything we DON'T want in our lives, allows us to make more room for all the things we do want.

The Guy Who Turns His Garage Into a Man Cave

Now don't get me wrong; a real man's man, someone who's hardcore into sports, loyal to his favourite team yet still deeply devoted to you, and actually takes you to a Raptors game when he says he will, works. Although I'd rather be having eggs benny and spicy Caesars at the Four Seasons Hotel on a Sunday afternoon with a metrosexual instead, someone I can down a few beers with when it's his turn to host game night, in a finished basement I might add, is okay too. The dude hooking up his 27" TV to garage drywall, purchasing a fridge and used couch off Facebook Marketplace, spending an entire day where his car should be parked, is not. This brings us to Post-It Note #1. This guy is not only hiding from his wife, children, and responsibilities, but also from life itself. And a decade later, after the marriage is over and man cave is gone, the only thing that will have changed is location. Trust me. The day-drinking, recreational weed use, and six-hour online *Texas Hold'em* marathons, regardless of where, will always come first. But if he had just come inside the house or pounded the pavement looking for real work, rather than wasting his time on a dirty concrete floor, who knows where he'd be today?

The Guy Who Keeps a Tent in His Trunk

I've always said, it's way easier to be with a guy who's your equal than one who is not. This means someone on the same level, who's motivated, goal-oriented and wants to succeed in life. Perhaps he even owns some property, as I already do! Instead of taking my own advice, I ended up dating the schmuck who keeps a tent in his trunk 24/7 so he has somewhere to sleep, or correction, sober up, whenever he drives up north to party at a buddy's cottage. But I want the man who owns the cottage, not the mooch who's already experienced waking up naked on a floating dock with hungry seagulls perched on his head after a night of debauchery at a more successful friend's place. Thankfully, this freeloader and I ended things before our summer season began, which saved me from having to accompany him on any of these last-minute (he isn't a big planner) excursions. But, if you're a hard-working and deter-mined guy who's already purchased your dream home in Mus-koka or Balfour Beach, even if with a little help from your parents (like every other Jew I know), I'm in. Because I already backpacked through Europe decades ago, and I have no plans on pitching a tepee and crashing with my boyfriend on a bro's 10-acres anytime soon.

The Guy Who Rents an Apartment with Parquet Flooring

If I'm coming across as judgy with this one, I'm sorry, not sorry. But experience has taught me to stay at least 100 meters away from any man wandering through life on parquet floors. Post-It Note #3: he's struggling more than he's letting on. And most likely he doesn't own a dishwasher, a washing machine or a dryer either. One thing's for sure—I'm done with renters/tenants. So, if you're still waiting for the housing market to crash so you can finally get in the game, or you're investing what little cash you have in Bitcoin, you can continue paying someone else's mortgage with zero equity of your own, without me. Do I get that we're not all in the same situation in life? Yes. But when I was living in a beat-up old building with ugly, tiny square wall-to-wall woodblocks and my two cats, I was 20 years old. Not a grown-ass woman. However, if you've recently separated, are paying way too much in child support, contemplating your next move, and love expensive dark hardwood, I'll make an exception. I'm not a complete monster! If you're still writing monthly cheques (after a decade) for that damaged century-old, mass-produced unit with scratched up fake French floors, and you haven't gotten your shit together yet (like tent guy), chances are we've got different ideas about where we want to lay our hats and what constitutes a home. Side note: vinyl and laminate flooring are a definite grey area, but most likely a no-go.

The Guy Who Won't Fuck Us on Our Period

Are you a "lay down a towel or New York Yankees tee" type of guy, or a "wait four to five days for the bleeding to completely stop" kind of man? Because if you're willing to get down and dirty with me, whatever day of the month it is, that's the only Richard or Harry I want. Period. And although some of my male friends swear it's the other way around, with their girlfriends being the ones refusing to re-enact a crime scene while on the rag, from my mouth to your dick, I'm so not that girl. Instead, I'll send you a text of Tom Hanks' bloody best friend, after you've just WILSON'd my leg. And although I've been known to get a little psycho around my time of the month, so much so that the last guy I dated had to mark mine down and keep track, it's a proven fact that women are way hornier on their periods and even wilder in bed. Lucky for me, the majority of my boyfriends haven't cared, even the one running downstairs to his basement laundromat to wash (and air-dry, obvs) stained sheets. Although I'm guessing the guy who forced me to use sanitizer once before giving him a handy in his Beamer (pre-COVID) wouldn't agree. So, if the thought of menstrual blood on your junk or a few droplets on those gorgeous parquets makes you feel faint or queasy, please take your juice box and cookie and be on your way.

The Guy Who Isn't Quite a Straight Shooter

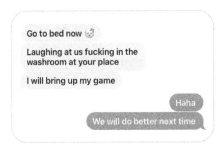

Go to bed now 😴

Laughing at us fucking in the washroom at your place

I will bring up my game

Haha

We will do better next time

Let's just say, the guy who's reaching for the pink Bella Silicone G-Spot vibe every single G-ddamn time it's our turn, is lazy AF. Do you want a Sexypringle or not? I need mad skills to keep this thing going. So, find out what we like. Make more of an effort. It's not that hard. Especially if you plan to be.

The Guy Who Says "Let's Take This Outside"

Dating a brave and self-assured cave man in the prehistoric ages was obviously imperative for women's survival. Nowadays, though, we can easily select, access and independently pay for our own dry-aged meat at Barberian's Steak House. So naturally, our selection (see what I did there Darwin?) when choosing a partner isn't dependent on a man's ability to flex anymore. Therefore, dating a brute, whose first instinct is to suggest stepping outside if someone looks at him the wrong way at a bar, intentionally waiting for the other guy to throw the first punch so he won't get charged when the cops arrive, is pointless. Welcome to Post-It Note #6. This guy has always been an archaic mess, even needing emergency dental surgery in Florida when he was 18 years old after pissing off a drug dealer who knocked out all his teeth. Um, did he not get the memo? Grown men don't physically fight their own battles; nor should they ever attempt to build their own backyard deck! They hire people to do that shit for them! Today it's all about finding a guy who can resolve conflict without violence, and only steps out of a bar when it's time to take me home.

The Guy Who Smokes the Minute He Wakes Up

You were gross. 'Nuff said. But let me elaborate further. Dating a guy who lights up a cigarette the minute he gets out of bed in the morning, or better yet, while he's on the toilet taking his regularly scheduled morning dump (turning on every fan in the place so his sleeping kids don't catch on), is someone I will never love again. No girl wants this. Ever. So, for all you Julians, Rickys or Bubbles out there, supporting a two-pack a day expense, jaywalking across the busy main street to Sev Lev in the dead of winter in just a wife-beater and flip-flops, the *Trailer Park Girls* are that-a-way. I grew up on

I only have a couple butts...if you don't have a lot could you PRETTY PLEASE stop and get some. Woot Woot

If you don't want to obviously I walk across the street

Gonna take a bath now

Of course! Just text me what you want i got it wrong last time

Small regular duMaurier Signature...

Thank you

the other side of the track, remember? Couldn't you have been like everyone else I've dated, lighting up only when we are drunk or high? Or more like the guy who puts on his Nike Airs and goes for a real run, instead of sprinting over to the convenience store in them? Because this is the kind of man I need. Thankfully, hardcore guys like my ex who smoke 24/7 are now a dying breed. And finding someone to burn through my "break glass in case of emergency" stash immediately following a few martinis, rather than jonesing for that third pack at 1 a.m. after a few too many *Cuba Libras*, is much easier to find.

The Guy Who Gets Drunk at a Shiva & Video Chats You

Everyone including LL Cool J knows that being with a guy who "drinks too much and smokes too many blunts" isn't smart. Except for the guy who gets shit-faced at a Jewish Shiva. Which, for those of you who don't know, is a week-long mourning period in Judaism that takes place directly after a burial/funeral. Rather than being a man of integrity, or a "mensch" as we Jews like to say, and providing the grieving family with a Kosher hot meal, my boyfriend would bring Chivas instead, FaceTiming me from inside their home as he pounded back shots. But the man in the background wearing a kippah and eating mandel bread while sipping on a coffee and consoling Bubbie is the person I should have been focusing on instead. Because dating a guy who's inappropriate 90% of the time, and who encourages his friend's 15-year-old nephew to get plastered with him during a live Zoom memorial after her father just died, isn't someone to grow old with. He's the self-proclaimed Cabana Boy at a pool party, the Fluffer on a porn set, or the Hype Man before the main act. Always laughed at, but never with. To this day, he still has no clue that people even perceive him this way. There's a right time and a right place for everything. It's important to find a man who knows the difference.

The Guy Who Goes to University but Fails to Graduate

My intent isn't to knock anyone down who hasn't gone to university or college, since there are plenty of successful guys out there who have made it without that particular piece of paper. *Fuck a PHD, I'm still hoping for a MRS title.* Mark Zuckerberg and Bill Gates, for example,

both dropped out of Harvard to pursue their dreams. Even Richard Branson left high school at 16 years old and is now said to be worth 1.4 billion. It's the loser who's smart enough to get into university, and fortunate enough to have parents willing to pay for his education and the apartment he rents with a bud, but who pisses it all away, that we need to watch out for. Don't get me wrong; I too partied my ass off, missing lectures and killing brain cells during my stint with higher education, which is par for the course. But I also knew when it was time to buckle down, and I graduated with an Honours BA in Anthropology and a second degree from Seneca College in Radio and Television Broadcasting. My ex, on the other hand, only passed three courses the entire time he was there. You heard me correctly . . . only three damn courses! So, if you ever find yourself in a situation such as this, drop out of the relationship immediately and find someone who knows how to properly finish.

The Guy with 99 Problems

Have you ever dated a guy with "99 problems but a [bad idea] ain't one?" You know the guy; the one who's always searching for his next big break, but never follows through with anything? Like selling weed in sealed tuna cans, which by the way has already been done. The man who spits on every opportunity he's ever been given, directly in its face. Well, I ended up dating a man exactly like this, although I didn't find out about it until well into our relationship. Years ago, back when my ex was married to his ex-wife and working at a large, high-profile corporation, he got caught without a university degree when HR conducted an employee check four months in. But instead of getting fired for lying on his resume, or as he puts it "withholding info they technically didn't ask for," they said he could keep his job and the six figures they were paying him if he just completed his university degree part-time, even offering to cover the costs for the remaining courses. Talk about winning the lottery?! But he quit instead. You heard me right . . . he passed on the incredible opportunity! So, ladies, the next time a man tells you on the first date that he's educated and has attended university and/or college you likely have no reason not to believe him. Most men are telling the truth and have no reason to lie to you. Continue to date number two as planned. However, if later in the relationship you suspect that you might have mistakenly chosen a failure like I did, ask to see his transcripts.

The Guy Who Hands You a Barf Bucket & Leaves

The bucket incident of '96 is something my good friend Marie, who I've been friends with since our Whiskey Saigon bartending days, still talks about. It involved a douchebag boyfriend who brought her home from a party, handed her a dirty pail to puke in, and then left her alone to go meet friends. Years later, I too was dating an inconsiderate, A-hole like this, except mine was a middle-aged man who'd toss me in an Uber minutes before last call so he could continue chasing his high. An improvement, though, from the Irish exits he'd pull with his past girlfriends, who he'd often bail on completely without ever saying goodbye. One night after flirting with me for hours over the phone post-breakup, he invited me to meet up with him and some friends the following day but failed to mention to any of them that I was coming. Not surprisingly, this, of course, made me look like a complete stalker once I arrived. He then left without offering me a ride home despite the fact that we only lived five minutes away from each other. It was his bud, rather than him, who messaged me on Facebook the next morning to apologize for their collective misjudgment and to check if I had gotten home okay. And although we weren't together anymore, nor was I his responsibility or even the friend he now claimed he wanted to be, it still stung to be treated this way, and it left me questioning if he was even worth holding onto. Am I a strong independent woman who can find my own way back home, even when tipsy and stumbling in my Louboutins (a girl can dream, no?), looking for a cab while randoms harass me on the street? HELL yes. But a true gentleman makes sure we arrive home safely. So, to all the guys out there who have held our hair back when we're face-down in a toilet, brought us a warm damp cloth for our foreheads, a glass of water and an Advil, or simply made sure we got home in one piece, thank you.

These are the men we should be spending time with, not the selfish Mr. Snuffleupaguses, who disappear into the night and only think about themselves.

The Guy Who Isn't Into Titles or Labels

We've all been there—dating men who won't commit. Unfortunately, my entire twenties were spent focused on DJs exactly like this. First there was DJ X, who wasted two years of my life, never once referring to me as his girlfriend. To the naked eye we were very much together, but behind closed doors I was just his naked fuck buddy. I even jumped out of a plane three times after he became a skydiving instructor, hoping this would bring us closer together. It didn't. I spent years afterwards hanging around DJ booths, casually dating whoever happened to be spinning. Then there was my boyfriend John, who I was with for a year when I was 30. But he only said "I love you" one time, after popping an E on Pride weekend. And when he introduced me as "the girl I'm bumping uglies with" to his sister on the night I was meeting her for the first time, I knew I wasn't the one. He *George Clooney'd* me shortly after that introduction and just one month before we'd planned a trip to Prague, saying that he never wanted to get married or have children. When he invited me out to dinner just a few short weeks after the breakup, ironically picking the same spot he took me to on our first date, I was convinced that he'd had a change of heart. But dinner was just a ploy to get me to agree to pretend I was sick a few days prior to our scheduled flight, and then ask for a doctor's note, just so he could get a refund on my plane ticket he had paid for. When he found out that I hadn't called my GP, he stood outside my apartment building (immediately following his return) ranting and raving like a lunatic, yelling my name, instead of "Stella's". And today? Today he's legally bound to another woman and the proud father to an adorable two-year-old baby boy, living the life he had adamantly claimed he never wanted. I guess it wasn't the life he didn't want, it was ME he hadn't wanted. But I digress. My most recent ex ended up blowing up at me when I referred to him as my boyfriend, which he most definitely was, during a phone call we were on after giving things another try last April. It turned out this time around he didn't want the title, proving just how serious he was about the reconciliation. This was confusing as fuck, since everything had pretty much gone back to the way things were before the breakup, and he had just asked me to Google "TV shows to watch with your boyfriend" a few nights prior when we'd run out of Netflix and Chill options. Of course I secretly took this as his way of letting me know we were back on track. But when I brought this contradiction up after he coldly informed me that we weren't in fact together, his excuse was "it was just a phrase Karen, and not meant to be taken literally." Really, brah? So, the next time someone says, "we don't need a label to define us," LISTEN. Until he's made his intentions clear, you are still single.

The Guy with Road Rage

Now don't get me wrong—I too have been known to flip the bird on a few occasions when someone inconsiderately cuts me off or drives extra slow on purpose when trying to make a point, but I've never side-swiped a car in a fit of anger. Not once. My ex-boyfriend, on the other hand, has a well-known documented history and reputation for doing dangerous things just like this. He even rang me up once, stressed out of his skull, because he thought the cops might show up at his door any minute and arrest him for driving someone off the road. You see, he's the guy who gets out of his car to "engage," even when statistics have proven that people get shot and killed for petty shit like this every day. He's the dude who rolls down his window to yell obscenities and insults at an asshole driver's wife or girlfriend sitting in the passenger seat. Is it ever worth it? Plus, outbursts like these may be hinting at a much deeper issue—one that often requires getting some help. Professional help. Luckily, whenever I was in his Audi, he behaved, honoured the speed limit and always thought about my safety first. His sudden outbursts, though, going from 0 to 10 in a matter of seconds or "HULKING" out every time someone or something pissed him off (on and off the road), should have been reason enough to leave. But this is how he lived his life, compulsively, making rash decisions and always reacting before thinking things through. So, it really shouldn't have come as a surprise to me that he treated our relationship the same way he approached conflict on the freeway. Note To Self: Find a calm and grounded man who isn't into drag-racing; maybe someone who dabbles in meditation, or yoga. More importantly, find a man who always lets the other person pass first.

(BONUS) The Guy Who Takes a Shit in an Aisle at Shoppers Drug Mart

Trust me, I'm not trying to sell more copies of the book with this one. One boyfriend did in fact drop his drawers at a Canadian pharmacy a few years back and defecate (I imagine in the Pampers section, ironically) after the manager told him he couldn't use the restroom. Holy Fucking Overshare. I did not need to know this about him. Like, ever. Why he told me this I'll never know. He thought it was hilarious. What's next, openly peeing in a community pool, or a Dutch Oven? "I showed him" he boasted, as we drove past the store where he'd dropped the stink bomb. "You saw *Bridesmaids*, right?" I joked, reminding him of the scene when Maya Rudolph gets food poisoning and takes a dump in the streets of Milwaukee. But my boyfriend hadn't eaten any bad chicken that day. He'd chosen to push one out on PURPOSE, just to prove a point to a retailer who'd pissed him off. A point only a baby wearing a diaper or the stars of *2 Girls, 1 Cup* should be making. Could he not have just shit in his pants in the privacy of his own damn car, like a normal person who can't hold it in any longer does? (GUILTY). If you're involved with a man who's actually capable of pulling a "clean up in aisle two" shenanigan in public, the real shit is coming soon. He's a mess you don't want to wipe up.

Chapter 8

What Sex With a Senior Citizen is Really Like

It's no secret to my inner circle, or anyone who follows me on social media, or anyone who's ever crossed paths with me, or anyone who will listen, that I dated and fell for a 65-year-old man who's now almost 70. Yikes! And although he turned out to be a grandiose, textbook narcissist, who often refers to himself in the third person, has a bookkeeper like my dad, owns a dresser drawer full of flannels, calls his cleaning lady "the maid," still reads the newspaper, and sent me a fake "sorry that was meant for someone else" text to spark jealousy, rage and confusion . . . our toxic relationship was extremely codependent equally on both our parts. It's precisely the reason why we dragged on for over a year. But no matter how many times we'd break up or hurt each other, we kept coming back for more. Was it the sex? Maybe. Which was dry as fuck at first. No pun intended. But this is a story I want to share, because it's the number one question I still get asked. So, if you want to know what schtupping a Jewish alter kaker 20 years your senior is like, because you just can't seem to picture it (I certainly couldn't before giving it a whirl), then keep reading.

Let's just say I wasn't surprised when he walked into d|Bar that first night in Yorkville. He was your typical short, fat, bald-ish, older Jewish gentleman. Basically, he was exactly how every hot guy I went to high school with turned out to be. But he looked to be about mid-50s in his profile pic, so I agreed to meet for a martini. And no, we didn't go to The Jolly Miller where he'd initially insisted on conducting the interview because this biatch doesn't do pubs . . . or Wet-Naps! And although we both ended up having a really great time that night (him more than me obviously), I certainly couldn't imagine getting naked with him. So I sent the obligatory "thanks but you're too old" text after finding out his real age, and suggested we just remain friends. And while he agreed that it was probably best to keep things in the friend zone since I was way too young and completely out of his league, he continued taking me to fancy "I clearly want you as my girlfriend" Toronto hot spots. And somewhere along the way, I decided why the hell not try being something more.

I'm not going to lie, the expensive dinners and over-the-top gifts early on definitely bought him some extra time, because he kissed like Woody Woodpecker, which was completely off-putting and not at all sexy. I wasn't sure if the short, annoying taps to my lips was something I'd be able to work with. Plus, when I went to his condo for the very first time, I discovered he had a real-life Regina George from *Mean Girls* situation going on, with a 14-year-old daughter running the show. "You sleep in a single bed because she made you trade with her?" I laughed. "How do you bring women here? How do you have adult relationships? Aren't you embarrassed? Who's in charge? How do you even fit in the bed?" I had so many questions. But instead of answering any of them, he quickly excused himself and announced that he had to go pee-pee (his actual words, I kid you not). Sex was the furthest thing from my mind.

Did the Generational Gap Make it Tooo Hard?

After a few months or so of PG dating, it was time to consummate whatever was going on, which for me was still just a "maybe." So, I got in an Uber after receiving the "I'm cooking you dinner" code text, knowing exactly who and what was about to go down that night. I'm not gonna lie, I was nervous, wondering if there was enough attraction for me to go through with the deed. Thankfully he had called "his guy" earlier that day, because there was no way I was getting through this on vodka alone. With my Spotify playlist streaming through his speakers (kudos to him for pretending to like rap) and a little substance courage, we moved to the sectional sofa, which was thankfully nowhere near his daughter's single bed. But when I put my hands on his (beef) knich for the very first time, rather than the usual responsive sounds I was used to hearing, I got a Woody Allen-esque commentary instead. "Oh yeah, this is nice. . . that's good, I like that. . . interesting. . . Oy my hip, wait give me sec, it's a kink . . . okay it's not a kink, I'm fine, continue, yes, continue. . . this feels nifty . . . thank you so much . . . thank you again . . ." with every stroke. And although it was weird AF, and I instinctively replied with a "you're welcome?", I was oddly into it. Our first time having sex was even more bizarre. He ended up pulling out mid-thrust a few seconds after starting, and leaving the room in a dramatic huff. "Did

I do something wrong?" I asked. "Yes, you're being too aggressive. Stop telling me what to do," he yelled. Apparently the Longo's cashier he'd been screwing for years before me was extremely submissive, and having gotten used to that, I intimidated him in bed. Poor fella. As the weeks progressed, though, we became more comfortable with each other, and it got better. Actually, it got more than better; it got amazing. The only problem was, he couldn't cum. Not ever. Do men even get this backed up? Where does it all go if not out? And since I'd never dealt with anything like this before, it was extremely uncomfortable and tough to bring up. When I finally did say something to him, he revealed that he was on anti-anxiety meds. "Oh, so it isn't your age," I blurted out. This was one side effect I was just going to have to accept.

Oldie But a Goodie

Now that I've had some time to reflect on things, as well as a few age-appropriate men to compare him to, I can confidently say that the sex was top shelf; we both couldn't get enough of each other. I know this is the opposite of what people expect I'd say with someone so old, but I truly loved having sex with him. Unfortunately the (bird) kissing never did improve with time, but he was skilled in so many other areas, particularly on his travels down south, that I didn't care. So would I do it all over again? Fuck yes.

And although there was an obvious age gap, which I was reminded of every time he ordered an onion bun at Bagel Plus, or spoke for that matter, he did eventually replace pee-pee with WAZ. Hey, not everything can be perfect, right? But he really was a FUCKING CHAMP between the sheets; always horny and grateful for the Premium P, had the stamina of a 20-year-old, rock hard every time, and never once complained that he was too tired, not in the mood, or needed Cialis. And trust me, I've had my fair share of limp-dicks far younger than him. The only compromise was never once having an orgasm together or watching him climax, which is a huge turn-on for me. On the plus side, he was able to penetrate me for as long as I wanted, and we finished only when I was done. If I had to choose an ex from my past to hypothetically revisit and fuck, the old man takes the win. Even more so than the much younger deadbeat I dated a few months later, who's now probably nursing a bruised ego with a *stiff* drink after reading this. But there is simply no comparison. Oh, and in case you're wondering (and I know you are), he did eventually get rid of that embarrassing single bed and upgrade to a teen-size double, which I enjoyed sleeping in MULTIPLE TIMES.

Chapter 9

How I Accidentally Became a Prostitute for a Month

. . . .

First, I'm going to preface this chapter by saying that no, I was never an actual high-end (obviously I'd be expensive!) call girl. Pleeease. Yes, I guess my behaviour during this brief period of my life was a bit hooker-ish, to say the least. But I'm not alone! Research has shown that there are thousands of women out there who are "open" to the idea of casually accepting gifts and/or money for sex, but would never admit this to their family or friends. Unfortunately for me, though, there isn't a sob story to accompany my foolish and slightly regretful stint. I wasn't in my 20s putting myself through college like a lot of modern-day sugar babies are, nor was I strapped for cash. It was just a fun, lucrative (or so I thought) way to pass the time, and a well-needed distraction as I was trying to get over yet another failed relationship. Or more accurately, it was the break I needed before running back for a hot minute to the senior citizen. Plus, it was empowering to take advantage of such stupid men who were willing to pay extra money for my time, on top of the elaborate expensive dinners and cocktails.

If you're wondering why I didn't just download Bumble or Hinge (thank you Simon Leviev and your "enemies" for turning me off Tinder), like all the other lonely singles out there looking for love, I did. But I wanted to try something I never imagined I'd ever do. So, I thought a platform such as this, with men who think it's totally acceptable to purchase women, and/or treat us like property or business transactions, might be fun. It also seemed like a sure-fire way to protect my heart, since they were basically all just a bunch of suckers I could secretly take advantage of and never take seriously. My main motivation, though, if I'm being completely honest, was just an excuse to clean up, go out and eat expensive steak. My monthly mortgage payments are taken care of by yours truly thank you very much, and I certainly didn't need a man to acquire, sign, and pay for a lease. But hey, if I could make my ex jealous with a slew of younger, hotter men, while posting it all on the 'Gram in the process, even better. Mission accomplished. So I signed up, found a somewhat dated and filtered pic to post, and got started. And although warning messages were plastered throughout the site ("Prostitution is strictly forbidden on WhatsYourPrice.com. Those looking for, or offering, prostitution services will be banned immediately and for life, with no exceptions"), let's be real.

Here's How it Works

Before a chat can even begin, money, which is used as an incentive to get an attractive woman to go out with you, needs to be agreed upon. Once an amount has been accepted? Let the shady corresponding begin. After weeding out dozens of inappropriate emails, and blocking every guy who sent a dick pic (News flash! We don't want to see it. Like ever), I met a couple of half-decent contenders. First up was an extremely good-looking gentleman from Hamilton whose name I can't remember (proving just how inconsequential he really was). He seemed normal enough; not creepy, just sad. Once we settled on $100, he agreed to drive an hour out of his way into the city to take me for dinner and drinks at STK.

It was the Raptors playoffs at the time, and he wanted to watch the game in style alongside a beautiful woman while eating oysters and sipping on Cristal. No argument here. And although I went into this never once treating any of 'em like proper dates (although with this guy I may have agreed to a second one had we met under different circumstances), the whole getting to know someone new, at a place I often went to with my ex, felt excruciating and made me miss my former more familiar toxic situationship even more. So in true Sexypringle fashion, I stumbled into the washroom and did what I do best. I sent a drunken 'I should be with my boyfriend tonight' text to the old man. To which he immediately replied, "and my girlfriend should be here with me, come over now." After checking my wax sitch, which was thankfully on-point, I went back to the table, said it was getting late, and used my son, who I knew was happily playing Roblox at home, as an excuse to leave. But as he was taking care of the cheque and asking when we could see each other again, which obviously was never going to happen, I started to feel guilty. In that moment I decided not to take the additional cash he was reaching into his pocket for and thanked him again for dinner. "No need to wait for my Uber, it will be here in a few minutes, but I'll call you," I said, as I kicked off my stilettos, shouted "bye," and started running in the opposite direction towards my ex-boyfriend's condo a block away.

Were the majority of the men I emailed and chatted with on the site just jackoffs looking for exactly that? Mostly yes. But there were also plenty of average, regular men too, who perhaps didn't have much luck with women, dating or relationships. Guys with no game, who thought they needed to pay an entry fee to get into the party. But were these guys any different than the dudes waiting outside Whiskey Saigon where I used to bartend, slipping our bouncer Tidwell an extra bill just to get through the doors? No. So maybe we shouldn't judge so quickly (even though it's hard not to. And yes, I'm fully aware that I too am being judged). And this brings me to my second date, who was in fact exactly this type of guy: paying a cover fee to gain access to my VIP table. Nothing more. A successful, intelligent, well-dressed investment banker, raising a 16-year-old daughter in Markham, yet completely unlucky in love. And I immediately knew after our first encounter that we would end up being friends. Based entirely on how we met, a relationship was out of the question, but today we continue to talk regularly. And although he did in fact pay me to sit and eat sushi with him on that first date, slipping $100 into my jacket pocket as we walked out, without me ever having to ask, he was the only person from the site who actually honoured our agreement (with cash) and never once treated me as a whore, even though admittedly I was acting like one.

Time to Shut it Down

My cue to permanently delete my WowGal1980 profile and get off this dreadful app happened on my third and final date, when the guy sitting across from me at Sotto Sotto looked vaguely familiar, like someone I might have grown up with. Turns out he was Jewish, grew up five minutes away from my parents, went to the same high school as I did, and seemed to vaguely recognize me too. When he asked for my last name so he could call his sister to see if she knew me, I wanted to crawl into a hole and disappear. I quickly flagged down the waiter and ordered us another round to distract him. OMG. So much for remaining anonymous! This role I'd been playing, similar to that of Mariah Carey's alter ego *Bianca* (only a true Lamb will get this reference) or Beyoncé's *Sasha Fierce* (for those who can't relate to Mimi) was about to be exposed. Had it occurred to me that people might find out I was on this shameful and degrading website? Not until that moment. And what started out as an easy way to grab some free dinners and dangle my goods in front of men who thought they had a chance, or enjoy a nice photo op to later torment my ex with, suddenly didn't feel right anymore. Later that night he sent me a "sorry I forgot to pay you" text, but promised to get me "next time around." Yeah, right, like that was ever going to happen. And in case you're wondering, he never did catch my last name.

When I got home that evening, I knew my escort-esque days were done, and I immediately deleted my account. I was tired of pretending to be someone I wasn't. And I wanted to start living a more authentic life. Maybe even find something real. It was time. Was it an interesting run? Sure. But I only met three guys and banked $100—what a complete joke. In the end I realized it wasn't for me. To this day I still get itchy hives whenever I think back or talk about this experience, even though I only partook in it a handful of times, didn't have sex with any of 'em, or treat it as extra income or a freelance side-hustle, like most opportunistic women on the site do. Plus, any dating site that warns "never send or ask for money or gift cards before meeting. Or share or request banking information. Report anyone who does" is far sketchier than I once thought.

Your One Free Hall Pass

Go ahead and label me. I'll accept it. You can even call me a whore to my face if you'd like because I definitely deserve it for signing up on this site and stooping so low. Trust me, it didn't change my situation, make me feel any better about myself (my self-esteem was at an all-time low at that time) or distract me from my sadness and loneliness, as I'd intended. I felt just as sad, just as lonely, and just as pathetic after every single date as I had going in. And the guilt? The shame? Let's just say, there's only a handful of friends I can openly talk to about this with. The other 85% don't even know. Did my sister beg me to remove this chapter from the book because of how bad it makes me look? What do you think? But the experience is a lesson learned and one I'm fine with sharing if it possibly prevents other women from repeating my mistakes. If you're trying to get over someone, move forward from a breakup, or distract yourself from being sad or lonely, there are more appropriate avenues to take to get past things, heal and move on—to that nice guy I'm hoping to meet offline. Perhaps my Rabbi knows someone?

Chapter 10

Here for a Reason, a Season, or a Lifetime?

. . . .

W hen it comes to trust and loyalty, my standards run pretty high. And although I've loosely referred to a few undeserving peeps over the years as "one of my best friends," throwing accolades where they don't always belong, I still know exactly who is and isn't deserving of this title. Take, for example, my BFF Joanna (AKA JoJo), who I met in high school when we were 16 years old. Three decades later she's still hands-down my number one fan. And although I talk to others more often than I do her, and waste hours on people not even half as worthy, she will always be my Blanche, Rose and Dorothy, all rolled into one. She's a lifer. *Schlemiel! Schlimazel! Hasenpfeffer Incorporated.* But these aren't the friendships we need to pay close attention to, or ever question. Everyone knows there's no Betty without Veronica, or Thelma without Louise. Squad goals!

It's the people who come and go, who don't always have our backs, and who haven't proven themselves yet, that we need to really watch out for. Because it's the wolves disguised in sheep's clothing, even if it's head-to-toe Gucci, that end up teaching us the more valuable lessons and make us appreciate our JoJos that much more. So, if you've recently walked away from a frenemy, distanced yourself from someone who's disappointed you, or decided to rid yourself of toxic and drama-ridden train wrecks, remember this: not every friend (or romantic relationship) is meant to be around for a lifetime. And the ones who come into our lives for a reason, or a season, are just as important because they often teach us the more valuable lessons.

Friends Will Sometimes Talk Shit About You

My earliest memory of phoniness from someone who I thought was my friend happened at summer camp when I was 11 years old, by a girl named Rebecca. After inviting her to my birthday party, her "sorry Kare, I won't be able to make it but hopefully I'll see you soon" RSVP on my answering machine didn't cut off when she intended. The "yeah but hopefully not too soon," that I also caught her mumbling under her breath while she LHFAO was also recorded by mistake for my impressionable ears to hear. Still, after responding with my own "maybe next time you should hang up the phone properly first" message on her answering machine, I'm glad I didn't end up taking things too personally, or ban her from my life forever. Because the reality is, sometimes friends talk shit. Or they diss each other. Or they bail on a party. It happens. It doesn't mean there's no hope for any kind of friendship. You might just need to redefine what that friendship is to you. Because after we both grew up and moved past our childish tiff, our weekly York University Underground nights (where all the first-years drank) really did rock. Today, venting about a good friend is just a regular Tuesday night. But I'll never utter anything behind your back that I wouldn't say directly to your face either. The mishap with Becky taught me this early on. Case in point: when a good friend was randomly hooking up with Tinder dates during COVID lockdown, but then wouldn't hang out on my balcony (socially distanced of course), claiming that it was "unsafe," you can bet your ass she got a mouthful from me, on top of the group text I sent out later that same evening calling her out. The Takeaway: Side-convos, not to be mistaken with side chicks, are A-okay in my book; they're part of growing up, and not worth severing any ties over. But only after you've called a bitch out of course!

Secrets Worth Keeping in The Vault

Sometimes, regardless of how juicy a secret is, you keep that shit locked up tight until you decide to write a book, and then it's fair game. When we're teens in high school, the bonds we form and the trust we build with our friends is everything. And although these friendships don't always last past graduation, it should be bros before hoes and sisters before misters, always. Right? Unfortunately, the reality is that this isn't always the case. Take my ex-boyfriend, for example, who called up the front desk and cancelled a friend's 7:30 a.m. hotel wake-up call while vacationing in Florida at 18 years old, just to be petty (see, he really has been an A-hole his entire life!). And 30 years later? The kid who missed his flight has never forgotten it. After hearing this story straight from the horse's mouth (we connected on Facebook) and then later confronting my ex about it after we briefly got back together, he lied and swore up and down that he had nothing to do with it. To this day, no one from that once tight-knit group of friends even talks to him anymore.

Luckily for me, when I was in high school, my girls were solid, and petty and cruel shade like messing with each other's early morning routine rarely happened. If it did, we never made it public knowledge. When we all decided to sneak into a male strip club for my birthday one year, with fake IDs discreetly hidden in our bras so our parents wouldn't catch on, what happened next, although epic, remained strictly between us. Needless to say, when Magic Mike came by our VIP table and started paying more attention to my friend Melanie, when it was my own Sweet 16, I was secretly jealous. Did our adolescent jaws drop when we saw his greased-up schlong so up close and personal? Fuck yes. But after he straddled Melanie's chair and brushed his junk up against her cheek, my jealousy quickly faded and I sipped my fuzzy navel for the remainder of the act, relieved I was a spectator instead of a participant. The next morning when we met at our lockers to "rock, paper, scissors" who was going to the mall to develop our Kodak FunSaver disposable camera, we knew it couldn't be Mel. Why, you ask? Well, the embarrassing bright red bumpy rash on the left side of her entire face told us so. "Guys, it's not what you think. I had a bad reaction to my skin cream last night," she cried in embarrassment, so we immediately dropped it. But not before teasing her a bit and offering up my mum's Rosacea cream for "mystery" irritations. And although none of us (except for me and JoJo) are even friends anymore (which is why I'm okay revealing this now), at the time we didn't tell a single soul about it, protecting her reputation in the process. My ex, on the other hand, has been a dick (not to be mistaken with the one that kissed Mel's face) his whole damn life, with a past that still seems to follow him wherever he goes. The Takeaway: Our actions, regardless of how old we are when we partake in them, have consequences. If we play nice, the universe will reward us with solid friendships, a (squeaky) clean reputation, and peeps who will keep our secrets safe (most of the time, that is). Because if any of us were to ever see you standing outside of a Chippendales show, we would all still warn you to avoid the front row at all costs!

When it's Time to Walk Away

Shortly after having my son, I began making new mom friends. But forming real, lasting bonds with these women proved more difficult than I expected, since having pushed a baby out of our coochies didn't necessarily mean we had anything else in common. Plus, sitting cross-legged in a semi-circle on a basement floor with mostly nannies (yes, I do live in *that* neighbourhood), singing 'The Wiggles' with infants who can barely hold their own heads up, was never really my thing. But every once in a while, I'd meet someone on the same page. Take Leslie, for example, who introduced herself to me at the hip hop dance class we both signed our four-year-old boys up for. We ended up sharing a lot of things, including a super-chill parenting style, holiday drinks in early November (obvs) smuggled in our Tim's dark roast while the kids were enjoying Gymboree, and even a knack for dressing up the boys as fairy princesses on Halloween to give all the disapproving moms something to really talk about. I recognized that instant connections like this weren't common, so when I met another mom, Sara, who was a freelance writer like myself, at the daycare our boys attended, I was thrilled. I even got her a job at Target Canada where I was working at the time, after my boss asked if I knew any editors. But when they secretly offered her my position, saying that they wanted to replace me, she never said a word and remained silent even after I confided in her over coffee that I was about to turn down another writing contract with RBC because I was happy where I was. Bitch, you knew my days at Target were numbered, so why not offer me a heads-up? When she did finally confess, the damage was already done and I'd already applied for EI. She ended up turning down my job, but it was too late. What I thought was a friendship, with some loyalty attached, was clearly not that. Her explanation as to why she didn't tell me landed on deaf ears, and that was my cue to leave, never to return again. The Takeaway: If friends don't have our backs, turn yours on them and run. Bye, Felicia!

This Fuck Up May Have Been Mine

When a 30-year relationship ends, no matter the circumstances, it's heart-wrenching. That's exactly what happened when I was forced to walk away from my childhood best friend, who I'd been inseparable from since Grade One. When she started making bad decisions and putting not only her own life in danger but mine as well, I wasn't left with much choice. It all started when she began working as a Toronto bail officer. After interviewing an alleged criminal behind a glass window, my then bestie, who obviously had some low self-esteem issues, began an inappropriate and unethical sexual relationship with the man she'd just granted parole to (an upcoming Netflix *Dirty John* season, anyone?). Now, this homeless drug-addict, who was also fighting the Children's Aid Society to get his three-year-old son back, was obsessed with and dependent on my best friend. And this stranger, who she had invited into my life without permission, knew my address and everything else about me. Plus, I'm pretty sure he was casing out my joint every time they came by. When I began to feel unsafe, thinking I might be murdered (he legitimately scared me), or that my kidney (you only need one, right?) might end up on the dark web, rather than talking to her about it which potentially could have become even more dangerous, I walked away from our lifelong friendship. I felt I had no choice. The email I received from her years later, though, describing me as an unsupportive, selfish friend who outright abandoned her, painted a very different story. "Bitch, I would have ended up in a body bag," I yelled back at my desktop. But too much time had passed, and I didn't know how to make things right, so I didn't respond. At the time I walked away, it was the right decision. She wasn't leaving him anytime soon and I decided to trust my gut. Do I miss her? Of course I do. It's been 15 years since we've talked. The Takeaway: Sometimes we need to bail on dangerous situations and set our ill-fated friendships free.

My Current Grey Area

Sometimes the decision to end a friendship or keep it alive isn't such a clear one. These grey area betrayals are tough for me, and it's a dilemma I'm currently dealing with involving a newish friend and my ex-boyfriend. Long story short . . . she's the girl who set me and my ex up, after he handpicked me from a Facebook post on her page. I, on the other hand, had no clue what I was walking into that first night, having agreed to meet him based on a profile pic which turned out to be footballer Len Dawson. In fact, his entire social media turned out to be a huge scam (possible red flag—what else was he hiding?) with not a single snap of him to use as reference, and his privacy settings purposely customized so no one could tag or post. Little did I know that this matchmaker friend of mine was about to hurt me too. But unlike my ex's predictable actions, her bitch slap I never saw coming. Turns out that her best friend from high school had been fucking

> I just texted him and said I don't believe him about the blond chick and he's probably fucking someone which is gross during Corona - I'm not even drunk and I can't help myself - what is wrong with me?
>
> Delivered
>
> Nothing but you need to let it go
>
> Even if he is with someone it's not your business cuz you're not fucking him anymore
>
> But if he is, he should tell you and be honest

him (see chapter: My Ex Left Me For A Trump Supporter) the entire time. I'm talking before we met, during our one-month separation before getting back together, and then immediately after our second and final breakup. And she never mentioned it to me. What was particularly hurtful was that after our breakup, when I still had hope that maybe we'd get back together based on his constant contact with me, blowing up my phone and claiming he was single, and not "dating anyone," my so-called friend knew all of this all along. Yes, you heard me correctly. She knew that he was hooking up with HER at the same time. For the record, I wouldn't have gone out with him in the first place when she first inquired whether I was single, let alone taken him back a second time, had I known about his history with HER. Gross. We are what we eat, am I right? Plus, I could have caught an STD (he wasn't into condoms) as a result of any crossover, or as I like to call it, double-dipping, which is only acceptable where chicken nuggets are concerned. I could have contracted COVID for that matter, since his booty call was known for attending secret underground parties (password entry required) and extremely large gatherings during lockdown. If he was willing to expose his own two children to a deadly virus by fucking someone so irresponsibly during a pandemic, my so-called friend, who'd been pretending to be my rock, should have protected me and my son by telling me what was up. Want to know how many times I called her up crying about a "mystery WAP"* coming and going from his place, who'd been seen by a friend who also lived in his building? More times than I can count. Instead of mentioning anything to me during these sob sessions, she'd have drinks with me at The Keg on

* WAP—Wet Ass Pussy, song by rapper Cardi B.

many occasions, look me straight in the eye and not breathe a word of what she knew.

Am I mad that she kept this secret? Hell yes. But I also understand what it's like when a lifelong friend tells you something in confidence. Still, she could have at least warned me, or given me a hint as to what was going on. Also, her constant calls and texts where she'd repeatedly bring up his name and probe me for info (clearly to report back to her friend) felt very informant-like, and

Karen, this is none of my business and it's between you and ▇ I hope this doesn't affect our friendship.

It doesn't. I just wish you would have told me if you knew thats all. You knew how much i was hurting. But its all good, I have no problem with anything or anyone

it's the main reason why I'm so upset. If she had just backed off, remained neutral, or avoided me and the horrible situation she'd been put in (anything other than what she did), I might have let things go. I'm trying hard to forgive my friend, because I'll be damned if I'm gonna let some cockroach and his menopausal sidepiece come between me and anyone in my crew. I'm failing miserably. I did learn this: not every friendship is black and white, and sometimes we should at least *try* to get past the complicated muddy areas and move forward. But it turns out, some betrayals can't be ignored, and not every friendship is meant to last more than a few seasons. Did I try? For a year to be exact. I didn't want to be responsible for breaking up a solid COVID bubble or force any of the other girls to choose sides. The Takeaway: Sometimes an apology is all that's needed to mend a broken relationship; other times it's not. For me, omission is the same as lying. Had she handled things differently, who knows. Today, the forecast remains mostly cloudy.

You Can't Force Relationships

My good friend Dan has an ex-girlfriend who's been trying to get back with him for over a year. And although he's made it abundantly clear that he's never getting onboard that crazy train again, there still seems to be some disconnect between his message and her understanding. Cue the 1 a.m. sexy lingerie pics. Honey, he ain't interested! And although your T&A look fucking fantastic, and intermittent fasting clearly works (noted), all he sees now is click-bait. The lesson here? You can't force relationships. And trust me, I've tried. Take, for example, media personality and former Much Music VJ and radio & television talk show host George Stroumboulopoulos, who I dated before his superstardom hit. And yes, I can totally name-drop here, and even give him a shameful plug, because we're still friends today. When I called him up one night at 2 a.m. after we'd already broken up, asking if I could come over to his place because I was scared and thought someone was breaking into my one-bedroom apartment, he agreed. *Yasss, I'm a fucking genius,* I thought, as I hung up my phone and immediately plugged in my flat iron. And although I lived on the fifth floor and the likelihood of a masked man smashing down my door was next to nil, he didn't once question my motives or make me feel stupid. Instead, he allowed me to crawl into his warm safe bed and fall asleep in his arms. Spoiler alert! We didn't get back together, despite my foolish attempts trying to make it happen. Nor did he use his ah-dorable brown puppy-dog eyes (have you seen 'em up close?) to hook up with me, which he could have easily done. Mad. Respect. Dude. But I digress, because it's these exact principles that we often use to measure relationships that should also be applied to friendship. Just like we can't force dudes from our past to take us back when something's run its course, we also can't convince gal pals to stay if they've decided to leave, or blow something silly way out of proportion. When my friend Jax chose to exit my life without my consent, after a ridiculous fight we had, I took it pretty hard. She was my ride-or-die, and her departure was a hard pill to swallow. But there's only so many apologies, texts or two-page emails we can send (or late-night robberies we can stage) before it becomes pathetic, and we just need to call it. With George, I learned this lesson the hard way, after years of highly creative failed stabs at another shot. Today I'm grateful for the friendship we still have, and I understand that people don't always remain in our lives forever (in the capacity we were hoping for). While there are some cases where we shouldn't give up without a little bit of a fight because they're worth it (Jacqueline was and still is one of these exceptions—as was George), relationships ultimately won't work if things are one-sided. I may still reach out to Jax just a *few* thousand more times before giving up entirely (yes, I know I have a problem with letting go, but I'm working on it. Baby steps), and I pray that one day we will resolve things and be friends again. But for now, I'm bowing out gracefully and concentrating only on the women (and men) in my life who continue to celebrate me, always. The Takeaways: (1) Always keep a baseball bat by your bedside for protection! (2) If the relationship ends amicably, he might agree to write your book foreword 20 years later! (3) You can't force relationships so stop trying. Those that are meant to last, naturally will.

Chapter 11

When Your Ex Keeps Throwing You Breadcrumbs

. . . .

The only present my ex-boyfriend gifted me the entire time we were together was a Bella G-Spot Vibrator. Turns out, he really was selfish and lazy! Although our date night outing to *Aren't We Naughty* to pick out our brand-new toy was actually kind of hot. And the sexcapades that followed. . . well, a lady never tells (although, who are we kidding? I subscribe to the TMI culture and will divulge every last detail if you ask). But just as things were getting deep (see what I did there?), he abruptly ended our relationship. The consolation prize? My returned magic stick, which we'd previously agreed on keeping at his place. Um, thanks?

News flash! Getting off is easy, and we all have options. Right?

Figures he didn't see the lineup of girls and guys all wanting to give me a try, so the parting gift was hella unnecessary. Regardless, I do admit I held off from diving back into the sex pool after we broke up. Because (1) it feels way too much like cheating if I engage in sex too soon after a breakup—apparently, he didn't agree; (2) past experience has taught me to avoid the whole "to get over someone, you need to get under someone" distraction; and (3) all the ambiguous breadcrumbs he kept sending me during those post-breakup months led me to believe we had a chance of getting back together.

Breadcrumbs? Really? I'm Worth the Whole Loaf

For those of you unfamiliar with the term "breadcrumbing," allow me to explain. Breadcrumbing occurs when an extremely insecure man who isn't ready to let you go strings you along, in some cases indefinitely, so that you always remain an option. It requires little to no effort, but just enough to give you hope. Breadcrumbing is also a common tactic used by narcissists who need constant ego boosts and a readily available supply of women at their disposal. Studies have shown that these men lack the empathy required to maintain healthy long-term relationships. Rarely does it ever have anything to do with you, and the cycle only stops once you finally decide to take action and end the back-and-forth games—which, clearly, I wasn't ready to do at the time. So when I received a text about a week after our breakup, after he specifically said there would be no contact, reminding me of a friend's birthday when he damn well knew I'd see the Facebook notification, and a later message letting me know that his best friend's

> May 29, 2020, 11:37 AM
>
> Hey hey...just saying Hi...and reminding you to look in your Louie...it's your best guy friends bday...woot woot..
> Hope you are doing awesome as always...

dad had just died when I had zero connection to her, I was confused. But I still took the bait. And I continued to answer the calls and texts that came afterwards, mistaking each one for genuine interest from him. Did my drunk dials ever go unanswered? Of course they didn't. Instead, he'd talk with me for hours. And although weeks would sometimes pass without any communication, he always seemed to resurface just as I was making progress moving forward. Once he randomly stopped by my place with a pound of corned beef from Centre Street Deli. Huh? Was he finally working . . . at Uber Eats, perhaps, after years of unemployment? Turns out it was just another breadcrumb delivery, minus the fresh sliced rye.

Another time he offered up an old mountain bike he had in his storage locker for my son. Had I been misconstruing these random gestures as signs of affection the entire time? Absolutely. When the excuses ran out, he began tugging at my heart strings, saying things like "I still have your toothbrush in my cup holder," or he'd flirt with me instead, remind-

Looks great.come and pick it up

That is great. Thank you...il call this week to come get it. Thanks again

ing me that the sexy panties I had (accidentally) left (on purpose) at his place were still in his bedside drawer. By now my friends were convinced he was a true sociopath and an even bigger dick than the silicone one he'd gifted to me. But in true Gretel fashion, I continued to ignore the reality of our situation, thinking that he must still love me or he wouldn't continue to engage, or keep offering to bring back my recycling bin whenever he drove by and saw it on the street. So, I kept reaching for the morsels of breadcrumbs that he continued to throw my way.

Take Your Cold Cuts & Shove 'Em

When a guy who knew my ex-boyfriend slid into my DMs to say that he had seen him with a blond woman in his building, I didn't know what to think. He was single after all, but he was also still talking to me for hours at a time, so I convinced myself that she must be just a friend. In some twisted part of my brain, because he was putting in so much effort to stay in contact with me, I still thought we had some unfinished business. I would soon find out the truth about this late-night mystery visitor. After confronting him via text about her (yes, I know, I'm highly reactive), his explanation was more about semantics than the actual truth. What I learned is that he had zero intention of ever getting back together with me, even though he'd

been feeding me false hope for months. His initial response to my question about her was that he was "not dating anyone." But a few days after receiving that text, I got an unsolicited call that would change everything. "Hey Kare, do you have a few minutes?" he asked, a question no woman wants to hear. "Sure, what's up?" He then proceeded to say, and I quote, "there's a difference between dating and fucking, and I like to fuck." Yes, he actually said this, verbatim. I was literally speechless, and

I couldn't wrap my head around the reason for this early morning mansplain. Why would he call me to tell me this? At this point he didn't owe me shit, so why hurt me? I certainly didn't have any proof of anything going on in his world, and the blond woman in question could have been his sister for all I knew, so he could have easily ignored my inquiry or left it at "I'm not dating anyone." "So, you're screwing someone else now?" I yelled. I acknowledge that it was unfair to question him at this point. He was single after all, although in my warped mind we were still figuring things out. "Yes, but I'm not dating, so stop accusing me of lying." *This is how it's gonna end?* I thought. What a dick move. I was curious about who she was, but when I asked, he wouldn't say, reminding me that I didn't need to turn it into anything that it wasn't. It was just a BOOTY CALL, he made sure to let me know. Wow. Just wow. The damage was done. He'd clearly made a conscious decision that morning to ring me up and stab me deeply, knowing exactly what the outcome would be. This was definitely not the action of a decent man, or one who had ever cared about me. And all those breadcrumbs he'd been feeding me for months were just unwanted carbs. It was clearly time to get back on Keto.

A Satisfied "KAREN" Returns Product Anyway

When it comes to how that morning started, let's just say I didn't complain to a manager or even ask for a refund. In fact, I was actually one very happy and (self) satisfied customer (and meme) after waking up with my Bella Silicone Vibrator, having finished just minutes before receiving the gut-wrenching call. So, what did I do? I *hot potato'd* my recently used dildo, plus some other things right back at him later that same day. Actually, my friend Havah did while I patiently waited in the car listening to their entire interaction as she secretly recorded it on her phone. A little psycho maybe, but only a silicone rabbit was harmed in the process (okay, Glenn Close?). Plus I'd just been penetrated pretty deeply; I didn't care about being sane. Finally putting an end to those long six months of living in limbo, I suddenly felt lighter. Bet he didn't see that cumming? Was I devastated? OMG yes. I had honestly thought we still had a chance at reconciliation, especially since he seemed unable to cut ties during those drawn-out months after we broke up. But it was never gonna happen, especially now that I knew her name, having found out a few weeks later who she was from a not-so-loyal friend of his. Guess that bro-code he always boasted about wasn't as tight as he thought. Today, the vibe's back at his place, I'm assuming in his nightstand drawer where it belongs, to use on the next girl he's unable to please.

CAUTION:
PLEASE WASH BEFORE USING

*(You might want to splash some soap
and warm water on it first. Just saying.)*

Chapter 12

My Parents Hired Me a Jewish Matchmaker

. . . .

W hen I was around 34 years old, I was forced to take action and seriously start looking for a husband. It was time to find a real man instead of the regular "alcoholics, workaholics, commitment-phobes, peeping toms, megalomaniacs, emotional fuckwits and perverts" I'd been drawn to in the past. I was single AF, and feeling very much like a real-life Bridget Jones at this point. So, when my parents decided to intervene and take it upon themselves to hire a Jewish matchmaker they had stumbled upon in *The Canadian Jewish News,* I thought, why not. "You already called and hired her?" I asked, pretending to be surprised that they'd wasted no time following up. "Yes, dad and I answered an ad." In their defence, they had just finished watching *Fiddler on the Roof.* So I messaged the matchmaker and we made a date to meet at a local area restaurant the following week. "OMG sweetie, you're absolutely gorgeous; stunning actually. Why are you still single?!" she shrieked in her yenta voice, pulling up a barstool while I sipped on a signature half-price Bellini trying not to get brain-freeze. This was her first mistake, and my biggest pet peeve when it comes to the questions that men, and apparently professional matchmakers, ask on a first date. But I ignored it and proceeded with my checklist. "I want someone who's never been married, has no kids, and is between 35 and 48 years old," I stated. Easy enough, right? A successful, handsome, tall drink of water, who's fucking hilarious, can keep up with me, and has a bit of an edge, was quickly added to the mix as well. I was still relatively young, so checking off all the boxes on my wish list seemed like a completely realistic and attainable goal. And all those deal-breakers that older women always seem to be compromising on? Well, they definitely didn't apply to me . . . just yet. Clearly, I had no idea what was coming my way. "I have an entire roster of men who meet your requirements," she was quick to offer, as she handed me the contract to date and sign, making sure her fees, and of course her very valuable time, were taken care of. Then she mentioned her two-drink max rule on dates (keep it classy), assured me that she'd soon be in touch with the first suitor, and quickly left. I was hopeful.

My advice for anyone thinking of trying this out for a standard one-year membership, at a hefty price I might add, is to read the fine print first. Because although it stated on her website that she guarantees unlimited introductions until you are married or in a committed relationship and/or minimum of six qualified introductions, whichever comes first, in my particular case this did not happen. All I ended up with was a handful of dudes who didn't match anywhere near the description of what I had asked for, and who I easily could have found on Craigslist myself. When I pointed out that every guy she pitched came with a *but* attached, she said I was being too picky, which I admit Jewish women are commonly known for. So, I tried to keep an open mind and trust the process. But as the months progressed, all I got was Absolut rather than the Grey Goose I was promised. Today, she's charging upwards of $10,000 to what I'm sure are sad, lonely men—the only ones crazy enough to pay that kind of cash. And I'm still single. Apparently, she still doesn't do her research, as I recently found out that she tried setting up someone I know with their very own ex-husband! Should I have stayed on Jdate, giving all those lifers (who to this day still roam the site) a chance, instead of putting all my eggs into one soulmate's basket? In retrospect, maybe.

Every time my matchmaker called saying that she'd found me a perfect match, upselling someone who was literally the complete opposite of what I wanted, I'd immediately hang up and start scrolling through Kijiji for cats. Clearly, we weren't off to a great start. That 80% success rate her website boasted about was starting to feel like a Ponzi scam. Because every introduction she made came with a compromise. When your matchmaker spends their time trying to make a convincing argument, rather than letting her products speak for themselves (ending every call with an "I know he's not what you want, but you should go anyway because you just never know"), that's a huge red flag. But I was, and still am, a hopeless romantic, so I agreed to every set-up. The first guy, Howard, had three small children and a dead wife. Yikes! And although he was great and we both had a nice time, I wasn't interested in going there, especially when having a biological child of my own was a top priority. The second guy, Jeff, who was the owner of a prominent downtown nightclub and hotel, 20 years my senior, and rumoured to be gay, rolled in wearing his signature blue-tinted sunglasses, keeping them on the entire night even though we were in a dimly lit bar. Did I remind my matchmaker when she called with his info that he was too old, and nowhere near the age range I'd given her? Yes. But she'd persuaded me into going, saying that he had tons of money and was a really good catch. She failed to mention his already well-known reputation within the Jewish community for dating much younger women (and men), including married ones. During our date, after he mentioned that he woke up every Sunday morning at 5 a.m. to read the morning paper, drink espresso, and eat Montreal-style bagels with lox and cream cheese, I knew he wasn't for me. Five in the morning was usually the time I'd just be rolling in and going to sleep! The next guy I went on a date with gave me a bit of a startle when he got up from the table and revealed his height, which I hadn't been made aware of. I legit felt like Liz Lemon in *30 Rock* when she briefly dated actor Peter Dinklage (huge character, small stature) after mistaking him for a child. Five-foot-one was a wee bit short, even for me, which is why I'm guessing my matchmaker left this tiny detail out. After a few more months of complying with her unsuitable setups, I finally dialed her up and politely asked for a full refund. "Nope, can't do it" she said. You went out with all of them and my fees are based on a few qualified introductions. "You said the ones I didn't want to meet with didn't count," I responded emphatically. After some back and forth fighting over email, which included a threat to write a scathing *National Post* review (this was pre-Twitter and before Yelp was relevant), she finally agreed to give back half the total cost my parents had kindly paid. In retrospect I probably should have cited the paper we initially found her in. I didn't hear from her again after that, until I received a random "are you single right now" message from her 10 years later, through Facebook Messenger. Needless to say, I dismissed her message, just like she had dismissed my desired criteria so many years before.

Although I never did meet my perfect match from that half-page ad my parents stumbled upon in the newspaper, or through anyone else for that matter, and my luck with men has always been similar to choosing the wrong briefcase and then rejecting the counteroffer in Howie Mandel's *Deal or No Deal*, I ended up doing something even better. I put my plans to wear that white dress on hold, and I decided it was time to have a baby instead. You don't need a king anymore to get yourself a little prince (or princess), just a good doctor! I dedicated the next several years to raising my little mensch on my own, while enjoying a few fuckboys on the side. For the most part this worked out just fine, plus I was simply too busy being a new mommy to start looking for love. But when my son was about eight years old, the matchmaker I had dismissed years ago suddenly popped up again, inquiring about my single status. And I let her back in, since I was now ready to start my exhausting search once again. It seemed less daunting having some help (even bad help?) than going at it on my own. This time, though, she was working for someone else, and I was just the bait she was dangling in front of her client. The suitor was an older gentleman looking for an attractive younger woman, and apparently I had quickly come to mind (yes, I'm that unforgettable!). I imagined her giving him the same "of course I've got tons of girls like this" spiel that she had recited to me almost a decade back, enticing him to sign on the dotted line. And that client who I ended up reluctantly agreeing to meet on that fateful night at d|Bar? He was none other than my 65-year-old ex who I speak about in almost half of this book. Can anyone say full circle? We were together for over a year, and this inferior matchmaker was verklempt with joy, and excited to finally get paid, match made. The question now is, do my parents owe her back that half refund she gave us all those years ago, even though we didn't end up getting married? Ha. Just like the hue of the hair on most of the men she used to set me up with . . . it's a grey area.

Chapter 13

When Your Body Rejects Your Boyfriend

. . . .

Typically, the only warning signs I've ever received when wasting time with a multitude of wrong men have come from my gut, hidden away in the pit of my stomach only to be completely and utterly ignored. Every. Single. Time. Surfacing after it's too late, when I'm either in too deep, or things are blowing up in my face, or I've received one too many "girl I told you so" texts from my knowing friends. I take full responsibility for my past mistakes, and I'm now working really hard to deal with all my unresolved issues from my past relationships, my apparent need to self-sabotage, and that voice inside my head that is constantly telling me that I'm undeserving of love whenever I meet someone new. I've made quite a bit of progress so far, and coupled with some of my more recent mistakes like the ex I've gotten back together with more times than I care to admit, and all the hours I banked putting up with his bullshit, I now know what an unhealthy and toxic relationship and person look like. But before gaining all this newfound wisdom and experiencing these revelations, back when I wasn't listening to my intuition (like I am now), my body decided to take charge and deliver my most painful message yet: I started having the most excruciating, debilitating, and sharp headaches whenever I had sex. These headaches felt more like brain aneurysms, which surfaced every time I was just about to orgasm, continuing up until it was over and then for hours afterwards. Nothing puts you in the mood like knowing hours of debilitating pain is the price to pay!

When Your Body Has Other Plans

> What's going on now?
>
> Today has been a night mare beyond..you'll have to understand.. I think you will when I explain.. am doing my best .. I have a Machiavellian spoilt little jealous little teenage brat and a crazy ex wife all descended on me at 8 this morning and dragged my mother into it. As we speak my little brat is coming back from Aritzia with her friend and my ex is sitting in my living room. All because I have a gf..
>
> Come on..take charge. This is ridiculous. It's not even your week. What could possibly be going on since 8am? And why are you letting this happen? Why?

After almost a year of what felt like a game of *Five Nights at Freddy's*, hanging out at my boyfriend's condo, constantly getting into arguments and never knowing what horror lurked ahead, it seemed my body had finally had enough. It began to completely shut down and reject the old man every time we had sex. Even though we were both still crazy obsessed with each other and we kept going back for more, he was unstable and we were definitely not healthy together. And although to the outside world it appeared that he was the innocent victim in a toxic relationship, falling prey to a much younger gold-digging vixen (my Instagram posts didn't help), all the torment he'd actually been putting me through was taking a toll on my mental health.

When his ex-wife started creating problems for us (on top of the numerous attempts by his 14-year-old daughter to break us up) I thought she was just jealous. Typical. However, I later found out that for the entire duration of our relation-

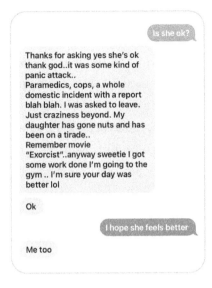

ship, he'd actually been playing us both, leading her on and giving her false hope that they might get back together, while downplaying whatever it was that he and I had. He even called her horrible names behind her back, to convince me that he was 100% over the marriage. When she finally confronted him about his false promises to her, and found out how serious he and I actually were, her body gave out on her too and she started hyperventilating, spiralling into a pretty serious panic attack. His terrified kid, who witnessed it all, called 911, and paramedics rushed to their house. When my ex arrived on the scene, his little girl began having a meltdown of her own, so the paramedics, who were now "legally obligated" to report any suspicion of domestic violence or abuse, immediately called the police. Statements were taken and my ex was instructed to leave. But his family blamed me for the incident (even though I was nowhere nearby), claiming that my presence in his life was causing everyone unwanted stress and apparently some emergency medical attention.

After this incident and a dozen more (including the time he went to an upscale restaurant we often frequented with a married woman who had slid into his DMs, and posted a pic on Instagram with the caption "switching it up," just to make me jealous), I was at my wit's end. We'd break up for a month or so, I'd go on a few horrible Bumble dates with other men, I'd start missing him, and then I'd go running back. It was a vicious cycle that kept repeating itself. And each time the cycle played out, it got harder to walk away. When he finally deleted the married woman's number from his contacts in front of me, trying to prove his loyalty, and promised to never speak to her again, while assuring me that the games would stop, I almost believed him. But a week later, after getting into yet another fight, he slipped and said that he'd secretly been talking with her on "WhatsUp." "You mean WhatsApp, grandpa," I immediately shot back.

Protective Measures

By now I had almost reached my breaking point, but I still wasn't quite strong enough to leave. So my body decided to step in and help me out (thank you?). It began to shut down and go into protec-

tive mode whenever we got naked. The first time I experienced the piercing pains in my skull, we were in the middle of having sex and I was just about to reach the Big O. Hearing my painful moan while I grabbed my head, he immediately jumped off me and ran to the kitchen to grab me a glass of water and some meds, thinking it was just a random headache. But the next time we were intimate, the throbbing agony happened again, seconds before I was about to climax, just like the previous time. This scenario continued every time we made love, up until the night I finally couldn't take both the physical and mental anguish any longer.

While the sudden migraines were anything but fun, they were an important wake-up call. It was like my body knew the end of our relationship was coming before my head did, so it began protecting me and taking the necessary precautions. And I truly believe that this was my mind's way of intervening to try and push me to find the strength to finally get me out of an unhealthy situation. By

> Please no guilt trips..I've been big about a lot of your behaviour. I've owned my behaviour.
> I tired to make you jealous admittedly.
> I went on some dates when we were broken up during the constant shifting cloudy status.
> I criticized you in an unfair way i.e your interests and intellectually..stuff like that. (yet I always said you had a higher I.q. than me)
> I see how unkind that can be and I apologize.

taking such a pleasurable thing for me, and one of the things I enjoyed most about our relationship, and ruining it, I think my body hoped I would get the hint that it was time to walk away. And it was the nudge I needed to finally break free. After sharing my epiphany with him and then announcing I was going to leave (think a "Dear John" letter, but in person), he retaliated by doing a pile of blow and interjecting a theory of his own: that he was much more intelligent than me and he'd never introduced me to his mother because I wasn't cultured or sophisticated enough, and "there was more to life than eating pricey steak and having manicured nails." But insulting my love for quality beef (dude . . . don't knock my medium rare!) was crossing a line. I was now ready to take the cues from my body instead and finally end things for good. And I guess my body

REALLY wanted me to listen, because magically, just like that, the pain ceased to exist once I had sex with someone new; disappearing completely as if it never happened. Now I'm back to enjoying post-coital smokes, not Tylenol. And today I'm left with a valuable lesson: always trust and listen to that little voice inside of my head, so that my body never hijacks my brain again.

Chapter 14

I Drunk Texted
My Ex Again

. . . .

S eriously, Sexypringle? WTF. Why all the drama after only two
of your signature martinis with blue cheese stuffed olives? And
what's with all the repeat performances? Even if it's five o'clock
somewhere . . . this doesn't mean you're good to go! Have I learned
nothing from my days as a professional crank caller in my 20s and
(sadly) 30s? Although my exes would describe me as extremely predictable when it comes to my "reaching out" tactics, even the most
advanced analytics couldn't figure out the algorithm behind some of
my most recent behaviour. Because frankly, it makes no sense. Even
to me. Case in point: my most recent drunk text, which was wasted
on someone I currently don't even like or respect anymore. And he
now thinks I'm an open candy shop, and all because I offered up
the Premium P (pussy) and hit "send," without using the Premium B

(brain) and thinking it through. The reality is, unless you're receiving propositions from a woman when she's sober, the joke's actually on you. Right? So why do smart, independent, educated and ridiculously sexy women engage in these self-destructive behaviours when there are still three seasons of Cobra Kai to get through? No clue. Because watching Johnny Lawrence get lit instead of inviting 'em over when we are is a way better call.

The Problem with Letting Go

Although I'm a strong and confident woman most of the time, the reality is I'm way too soft when it comes to love. I seem to forget all the times he automatically hit "on the other line. . . will call you back ASAP," suddenly treating me like an air duct cleaning solicitor when we used to talk 20 times a day. So, I hang on. And on. And on. But only to the good. And that's where the drunk texts come in. Ready. Set. Cue the vicious cycle. Because whenever I'm at a party or out with friends, and alcohol enters the (cocktail) mix, I end up missing [Insert EX Here]. (Please note: Names will vary over time.) It's equivalent to feeling homesick, and often results in calling an old boyfriend from the bathroom stall, or texting one directly from

the table for that matter, just to feel that familiarity again—even if you're on an incredible first date with someone else. Maybe it's just easier to go back rather than to start over. Whatever it is, if you're stuck in the past like I admittedly often am, there are steps you can take to recover.

For starters, stop blowing up his phone and sending mixed messages. Realize that moving forward is a process, and this process takes time. More importantly, though, remind yourself that it wasn't all good; there were disappointments in the relationship too. If things were as great as you're selectively choosing to remember, you'd still be together. Right? Lastly, if you're serious about ending those toxic late-night patterns of reaching out, you can delete these guys from your phone entirely. Am I there yet? Maybe not. But I'm close. And unless you're some kind of *Rain Man* who can retain digits by memory, the temptation to reach out will be harder to do. So, can I break free from my contacts and just call it a night? Let's knock back a few and see what happens.

Guidelines For a Serial Drunk Dialer Who Wants to Stop

- Know your limit. The number of drinks you consume will determine what comes next. For me, judgement, logic and reason leave the bar immediately following martini number three. Know yourself! If the goal is to keep things classy and not reach for your phone, make sure you know how much you can swallow before following the script.

- Alcohol ounces play a huge factor. If you choose to only have a couple drinks but they are high in alcohol content, don't be fooled. An average martini is three ounces per glass. Be aware of how many ounces you are consuming, so you can control any urges to contact that douche.

- Do not mix wine and spirits. Rookie move. The messier you get, the more likely you are to spill . . . your feelings.

- Live in the present. Concentrate solely on the people you are with. Whether it's a friend, a family member, a romantic interest, or some random buying you an expensive steak, enjoy their company instead.

- Do not groom or trim (on purpose). If the kitty ain't looking pretty you won't want anyone to see it, meaning you are less likely to place that call. (Side note: If you've got a pap appointment booked, immediately go to the basement of your nail salon; it's not fair to involve the gynecologist in your healing process.)

- If there's a "no electronics" rule at the dinner table in your home, honour it and apply this restriction outside. These principles shouldn't pertain to just children or the confinements of your own walls.

- Delete all go-to drunk dial contacts from your phone completely. If the ability to slip isn't there, the chance of contact lessens.

- Remind yourself of all the reasons why you aren't together anymore. Write them down in the Notes section of your iPhone. Then take five minutes to read them, instead of scrolling through your contacts searching for his number (which hopefully you have already deleted, see rule above).

- Hide your phone in a side pocket of your purse or shove it to the bottom where your tweezers, Altoids, old receipts and MAC lip gloss currently reside, to avoid easy access. Set it to "vibrate" for added protection (in case he calls you). This way you aren't tempted to make a drunk dial, but you're still available to answer the inevitable call your son will make asking if he can order Uber Eats whenever you're out on a date.

- There are apps that can help! Download Designated Dialer (for a small fee) which allows you to lock out certain contacts before you start drinking. If you try calling, you get a message reminding you of the mistake. Other apps force you to perform complex math equations beforehand to prove sobriety and prevent hitting "send."

- Take the whole *Designated Driver* and *Cock-Blocker* concept one step further. Designate a trusted friend to keep a close eye on your phone instead. Adding an extra barrier between you and your device means you are less likely to engage.

- Damage Control If You Slip: send a text the next morning apologizing for the late-night *Hotline Bling*. Blame the alcohol or, heck, pin it on your bloody period (works for me sometimes!). This (a) sends a clear message that you regret the contact, and that you obviously didn't mean it. And (b) his inflated ego is now back in check.

- Don't beat yourself up. Drunk dialing/texting happens. The next morning, take two extra-strength Advils, order the $4.99 "Big Breakfast" from Denny's with an extra side of sausage, sober up and carry on.

- When all else fails, deny, deny, deny. It never, ever happened. Right?

Hit Up Your Nightstand Drawer, Not His Phone

When I recently confessed to my friend Kimber yet another morti-fying drunk dial, she asked if he had a magical dick or some extraor-dinary skill I'd forgotten to mention to her. My answer was a Big Fat Hard No. For me, it's never been about the sex. *Whaaat?* Sure I'm a fan of great sex, but FYI: handing me a hanky after I sneeze, rather than a towel to wipe myself off with after *you're* done, means so much more. And if the relationship is already over, what exactly are we holding onto? Why do we turn bat-shit cray the minute there's a little vodka running through our veins? On top of the irrational behaviour some of us possess when it's that time of the month, or when there's a full moon. That's the million-dollar question, and the reason why my friends are on high alert and working overtime to distract me. But as time passes, though, I am noticing that the urges to drunk dial are lessening, which is certainly comforting. But that doesn't mean they've disappeared. I still have my setbacks after a few too many Grey Goose shots and end up sexting without thinking. So, should I take my own advice and delete the whole lot of them from my phone? Or join AA like the rest of the world and begin a journey of sobriety? Not sure. This is what I do know—every morning is a new opportunity to be with someone who hasn't cho-sen to exit your life; a chance to be with someone who chooses YOU. And every night we should only be playing with what's within reach. Note to self: buy new batteries. So stay tuned to hear about all the new messages I'll be sending out; messages to someone in person and in my presence, not over the phone. If you want to finally put an end to the vicious drunk-dialling cycle for good, practice safe sext and scroll through my rules rather than your contact list.

Chapter 15

Crying on a First Date, Who's With Me?

. . . .

I f it took me sobbing in front of a potential suitor, on a first date no less, to realize that I might have some unresolved issues from a past relationship (ya think?), then fine, I will call this spade out. Because I'm keeping it real, people. And that's exactly what happened. It was a real Sarah Bernhardt kind of night, with tears galore in front of a complete stranger. And at The Keg of all places, which is a painful reality for anyone who really knows me. Let's just say it was not a pretty scene. Nor was it comfortable for anyone involved: myself, our waiter, and pretty much everyone in the restaurant. Thankfully I was with someone who already thought I was adorable, even after the cryfest, and he wanted to stay rather than dash. So why all the waterworks, Sexypringle? And how does a girl redeem herself after such an embarrassing, very public, dinner-and-a-show? Were there reasons I couldn't keep my composure on this particular night, when I'm typically more of a master at fronting? Yes. With the luxury of some time, along with some reflection, I now know why.

Cheque, Please (And a Side Of Napkins)

The night started out like any other: fun, easy, and a ton of laughs. My approach to dating has always been positive. I love to dress up and go out, and I never treat 'em like G-ddamn interviews. Plus, a girl's gotta eat, right? So, after spending 20 minutes discussing why I won't order steak at The Keg (he didn't know my schtick yet), he began asking questions about my past relationships. I joked about how I accidentally became a gold digger (see: Chapter 2) for a year and tried my best to keep things light. "Wait, you dated a 65-year-old?" he choked. So I went into my usual spiel about that. When the calamari finally arrived, I dove right in, trying to soak up all the vodka I'd just consumed on an empty stomach. But it was sadly too late, because the minute he asked about my most recent heartbreak, a flood of emotions I'd been suppressing for months finally surfaced. I was beyond mortified at the poor timing of it all. Crying in front of a guy I actually liked was not part of the plan. But I couldn't help myself, and trust me, I desperately tried. It wasn't until I got home and replayed things over in my head that I realized my tears had nothing to do with sadness, loss, ego, or even my actual ex, and had everything to do with my own unresolved issue of not having understood the reasons for the breakup.

When it Happens Out of Left Field

Not being able to wrap your head around the real reason for a breakup is a hard pill to swallow. It can make us crazy and propel us to do embarrassing things. Like, for example, bursting into tears on a first date. But when a guy you've given your heart and loyalty to discards you like yesterday's trash, for reasons you know nothing about, it's an extremely difficult thing to accept. And trust me, it's not like I didn't ask him why. When he told me that he loved me during a morning cuddle, and confided that he'd never said that to anyone as quickly as he had with me, I believed him. And I felt it too, x 1,000. This was the real deal; the big Kahuna; my future. Or so I thought. But when things abruptly ended, coincidentally just three days after calling him out on his problematic relationship with booze, and some other questionable shit he had done, I was completely caught off guard. Most breakups don't just happen overnight or out of the blue. And when feelings change, there are usually warning signs that in retrospect we can say we saw coming. But in my case, I never received the memo. And to this day, we've never once talked about why things changed so abruptly and ended without warning; one day we were acting completely smitten with each other and professing our love and devotion to one another, and the next day he was done. I guess that is what I'd been struggling with for all those months following the breakup, and I guess that's why it finally surfaced that night over martinis. My brain had been working overtime to protect my heart from the pain and confusion around the sudden ending. Now that I have some clarity surrounding the situation (even though I never did find out why), I'm trying my best to move forward. So here's hoping for fewer tears and a heck of a lot more Billy Miner pie at The Keg in the near future.

When She's Just Not That Into You

To the guy who came along directly after my ex, my sincere apologies. Clearly I wasn't ready. But you really should have left me alone, given me more time to journal and meditate, or to get my retail therapy on at HomeSense, instead of coming at me full force with relationship dreams. The tears should have been your first clue that perhaps I wasn't quite ready. Hmmm . . . ya think? Still, I totally get your overeagerness to start dating me. I've met tons of men just like you, willing to take their chances pursuing a woman even if they know she's not totally over her ex, with the hopes of grabbing a piece of that pie. But chasing women who aren't over their ex is a dangerous endeavour.

Still Willing To Take The Risk?
Here's What You Can Expect:

- You will constantly be compared to the relationship we aren't quite over. Our memories are way too fresh in our minds. Although we will tell you, on repeat, that we are over it . . . don't believe us. We are not.

- Consider yourself lucky that we're sucking you off in the front seat of your BMW this early on. Take what you can get and lay off any talk about getting serious.

- Don't ask us what's wrong or send passive-aggressive texts pointing out that we're "acting pretty quiet" if we don't reply fast enough. Maybe we're on a mandatory two-hour User Experience training call with our work colleagues. More likely though, we're just deciding whether we actually want to continue dating you or not.

- We might receive a random message from the past, once the past finds out we've moved on (or attempted to). This will most definitely fuck us up for a few days, even if we know deep down that there's no hope of reconciliation (we already tried and failed . . .fool me once). So give us some time to process things and take care of any unfinished business. You're not out of the running just yet, so be patient.

- Don't push. It comes across as desperate.

- Do not suggest a cuddle. I don't cuddle or spoon this early on. Every guy I say this to makes it his mission in life to change me. Please stop. If you've won me over and I've given you my heart, that's a different story entirely. But I'm clearly not over my ex yet, so you'll have to wait (I promise it will be worth it).

- It will be months before we're ready to open up and trust again. So if you can't be patient, move on for now, save yourself the headache, and find someone who will offer laughter—not tears—with you on the first date.

Chapter 16

Go Ahead Ariana, Lick Every Donut

. . . .

I f men were like Timbits, we'd walk up to a glass counter, check out our options and choose the one that catches our eye. Right? Oh wait, that's pretty much an accurate description of dating, where we sample all the different flavours we're presented with until we find one to love. Remember when pop star Ariana Grande made headlines a few years back after getting caught on camera licking a donut on display, and then putting it back? Maybe it was the tiny taste she needed to help her decide before committing to the entire thing. But I'm the opposite: I'm the girl who holds on to the box of expired donuts, knowing they've all gone bad, getting her hands messy rather than trying a new one. That's a different chapter, though; one about holding on to things that have already gone stale instead of taking a chance with something new and tastier.

Most women crave a variety of options that they'll need to sample until they're ready to settle on just one. That's why I've put together a list of the top five Timbits to help narrow it down. But be careful when selecting your tasty treat, because you never know what you might end up with.

Funfetti When You First Meet, or Just Empty Calories?
(Birthday Cake Timbit)

This relationship is yummy from the start and it's a fucking celebration every time you're together. We're talking "hip-hop-hooray" vibes. He'll win you over with his funny(ish) charm, and just like that you're both all in. You've finally met something good to devour—it's the loot bag you want to take home. But when the party's over, will he still want you around? Nope. Surprise! You were just playing a game of musical chairs 'cause when things get tough and the music stops, his first instinct will be to walk away from that chair rather than attempt to win the game. He'll then bail and rebound with a cheaper, fully expired, messy baked good instead. Life isn't coloured sprinkles and sheen all the time. And a real relationship is about accepting both the good and the bad together. Which he won't. My advice: Pray that this Timbit never contacts you again and stops chasing that *Watermelon Sugar* high. His new flaky tart or cheap 10-pack he's previously munched on will satisfy his rush just fine. That's okay, because you've already tossed him in the trash with all the other "please play again" losers you've rolled up (the rim) and lost, and thankfully you've moved on from.

Not Worth the Stain on Your Shirt
(Raspberry Filled Timbit)

This flavour comes across sickeningly sweet at first, and charming AF. He'll make you feel like you're the most important girl in the entire world, but almost immediately, the relationship will take a messy turn. After you've reached your breaking point and had your last bite . . . boom, all the messy, sticky (jelly) shit from the centre will start oozing out. My advice: Run like hell. You're dating a selfish and entitled narcissist. Once he's been found out, everything will end up being your fault. He'll gaslight you, play champion jujitsu-level mind games, create arguments based on shit he's invented in his head, make you think you're crazy, and then discard you to find a new (bakery) supply in no time. And all you'll be left with is a powdery mess to clean up. Don't try to make sense of it all, because you won't.

The Darkest Vanilla You'll Ever Meet
(Chocolate Glazed Timbit)

There's something to be said about playing it safe when it comes to matters of the heart. Right? I've wasted many years of my life with the wrong kinds of men, seeking spice and danger, while mostly overlooking the safe Chocolate Glazed Timbit (thank G-d I'm still so young). But truth be told, this is the Timbit we should all be reaching for. Because with this guy, what you see is what you get, and he never disappoints; at least not intentionally. He's melt-in-your-mouth delicious. You're always on his mind, and he'll always put you first—even on his worst days. So, where's he been all my life? Well, for starters, not on any dating apps. He's the mensch your mom's loyal hairdresser sets you up with, or the guy you've had pinned to your Vision Board all along. He's even your friend on Facebook that you've never considered. He's all about family and honesty and, most importantly, you. My advice: Nibble on this one slowly and savour every minute, because he's freshly baked goodness and in it for the long haul.

If I Wanted Stale Bread, I Would Have Asked For a Crouton
(Old Fashioned Plain Timbit)

If there's more than a 20-year age gap, then he's probably a taste-less Old Fashioned Plain Timbit (not always, though; think Michael Douglas or Harrison Ford). But let's face it, do we ever really want this one? Sure, if your co-workers have grabbed the others first, or if you mistake it for a more flavourful option (AKA it's a set-up and you don't know his age). Unfortunately, though, he's dry as fuck, and after he orders marmalade on his toast you know this relationship isn't going down without a tall glass of milk. So, if you can tolerate stories from the '60s that will leave you feeling parched, then this is your guy. He'll be super into you, obviously, because you're full of life and he's retired and heading toward the end of his. P.S. He's not playing games, he just doesn't know how to text. My advice: If you want a boyfriend who reads the daily newspaper the way it was orig-inally meant to be read, in print, has a subscription to Toronto Life, and a handicap sticker for whenever you drive downtown (worth more than the vaccine passport IMO!), the Old Fashioned Plain is your top choice.

Home Sweet Home. You've Finally Arrived
(Apple Fritter Timbit)

What's better than the taste of warm apple pie? Not a whole lot. And ladies, with this choice you've found your husband. Where do I sign up? When you first meet, you can't keep your hands off this sweetie pie. You'll kiss for hours like you did back in high school. And he's super shy with you too, which is adorable. Outsiders are secretly jealous of what you guys have, and you're publicly smitten and Insta-approved. He's always kind, warm, and loving towards you, and he would never think of cheating—even in a different area code. Why? Because you're the centre of his friggin' universe. My advice: Just like the Chocolate Glazed Timbit, he's a keeper, so go ahead and enjoy this savoury treat for the rest of your life.

Chapter 17

Which Sexy Pringle Do You Want? (The Men's Turn)

. . . .

If women were like potato chips, you'd walk up to the chip aisle, check out your options, see what catches your eye, and pay. Right? The same goes for dating. Please note: (1) access to a flavour usually entails buying and eating the entire can; and (2) it might take you a long time to make a selection, since there are so many different options to choose from. And although some men have already found their carb of choice and don't want the extra salt, others are still hungry and looking for that one perfect crunch to fill their craving. For these men, I've put together a list of the top five Pringle chips. Choose wisely.

Often Imitated, But Never Duplicated
[Original Flavour Pringles]

A relationship with this one-of-a-kind Pringle will scare the shit out of you. So be afraid. Be very afraid. 'Cause you've never met anyone like her—ever. She's the real deal and you'll instinctively want to settle down with her (which can be frightening for some men, particularly those with commitment issues). Trust the feeling and go with it. Different flavours will come and go, but this is the one you'll always be craving. Or at least, the one you'll never *not* be craving. She is anything but bland, so never, ever offer her any dip. She doesn't need it. She's a stand-alone woman and just perfect on her own. My advice: She's special, and she makes it hard to let go. Plus, she's the OG of all the Pringles, and she's here to stay. Cheap, artificially flavoured *Lay's* may have been fun in the past, but after tasting this one, snacking will never be the same—plain and simple!

Packed with Low Self-Esteem
[Buffalo Ranch Flavour Pringles]

She's not the relationship type. But she's always up for a one-night stand, even though she's technically never had one because she's fucked you twice! This flavourful Pringle is unpredictable, has lots of friends. . . with benefits (of course), and she comes with a ton of regret and HEARTburn in the morning. On your first date, you'll drink way too much, take her for a ride (bareback I might add) and then intentionally lose her number. But this isn't her first rodeo, and she's not going down without a fight. You are now a challenge. And she doesn't handle rejection well. She'll *67* your ass until you pick up, WhatsApp you to see when you're online and if you're reading her messages, and then use temporary Burner phone numbers as a last resort. My advice: Not worth the effort. Ghost this crazy Buffalo Ranch Flavoured Pringle and enjoy the real deal on Tuesdays: half-price wings dipped in signature homemade-from-scratch buffalo ranch salad dressing instead. You'll thank me later.

Leaves a Stain on Your Fingers, Not Your Heart
(Ketchup Flavour Pringles)

This artificial Pringle brings nothing to the table, yet she's always at the table regardless. She's got no standards, is way too available, goes with just about anything, and loves getting passed around amongst all your friends. Plus, she's always DTF†. An easy replacement for a while (a temporary guilty pleasure) while you try to get over the Original Flavoured Pringle you lost. But primetime gold she ain't. In the end, she's not hot enough to keep your attention long-term. And after she realizes that you're only using her "on the side," things will get messy. My advice: Find someone with a little more spice or go back to the OG flavour you actually want. It's time to stop squeezing these half-empty girls into your life. You've already got enough on your plate!

. . . .

* *67—blocks your number so it doesn't show up when you call, crank call or drunk-dial an ex-boyfriend.
† DTF—Down to Fuck.

Finally, a Plan Worth Sticking To

(Reduced-Fat Flavour Pringles)

At first you'll think this Pringle is superficial and high maintenance. But she's actually your healthiest option. Although her Instagram account is full of selfies taken at 45-degree angles and perhaps a little too much FaceTuning, she's got so much more to offer than you might think. She hangs out on swanky patios, puts on makeup to Netflix and Chill, and drinks vodka straight-up or on ice to save on calories. But once you break down her walls and find that heart she's so desperately trying to protect, you'll realize she is worth the weight. This flavour is actually full of substance and super fun to be around—so don't let the label on the can, or what you see on Insta fool ya! It's all an act. My advice: No restrictions needed with this one. Forget the diet, 'cause this relationship is all about overindulgence, 500,000 kisses, and more.

Fire Up the Grill, She's a Great Piece Of Meat

(BBQ Flavour Pringles)

This is the Pringle you choose to watch the game with instead of cheering on your team with the boys. Because she's your private half-time show ('90s edition), sitting on your couch wearing your oversized Rams tee-shirt and nothing else (obviously). And she's hands-down your favourite person to hang out with. A relationship with this tangy girl is easy, and there's never any beef, except for what's on the snack plate she prepares for you and your friends on game night. She's always down to order Bistro wings and chill at your place, the first one to grab the darts at the neighbourhood dive bar, and she will drink watery draft beer without complaining if that's her only option. My advice: This relationship is smoking hot. Enjoy.

Chapter 18

Why Allowing My Boyfriend to Track Me Was a Bad Idea

. . . .

Remember the original mobile phone tracking app *Find My Friends*, which was originally just a basic GPS safety feature that Apple provided? It was mostly used on iPod Touch by teens to locate their friends at the mall, or parents needing to make sure their kids weren't skipping class and driving their Acura Integras (yes, my two best friends both got one for their sweet 16) to Olive Garden for un-limited soup, salad and breadsticks like I used to do. But sneaking off school property for food rather than drugs (I didn't light up my first joint until after graduation!) made this whole concept of keep-ing tabs far less useful in those golden days of innocence than it is in today's harsher realities. Plus, smartphones and tablets hadn't even come out yet, so the concept of tracking and location services wasn't much of a thing. But that was then and this is now. And now is a hell of a lot different than then. And although today's tracking applications have certainly saved lives (think locating those injured in a car crash who can't call for help, or finding missing individuals who can't reach out), both men and women today are using it for purposes it probably wasn't originally intended for (guilty as charged!). Like the guy who needs to dominate his power and control over his alleged property and know where she is at all times, or the person using it to create jealousy and insecurity in a relationship, as my ex-boyfriend did. Warning: If you plan on misusing this app, be prepared for it to backfire.

What started out as something I thought might bring us closer together and keep us better connected ultimately turned out to be a colossal mistake. In fact, I would go so far as to say that it is one of the causes of our breakup. In the beginning, though, there was definitely something comforting about knowing each other's location 24/7. It made us both feel more secure and possibly more committed than we actually were. And although I didn't think much of it when he asked to add me to his contacts so I could share my whereabouts—he was already tracking his 14-year-old daughter around town after all—I really wish I had considered the consequences before handing it over without question. I had nothing to hide at the time, though, so I quickly agreed. I was even able to pinpoint exactly where he was standing one morning when he called and asked for help after finding an injured bird on the street. Unfortunately, our feathered friend didn't make it, which I should have seen as a sign of what was to come for us.

Let the Unhealthy Tracking Begin

This particular relationship didn't start out in your typical way, and the romance always felt more like an ongoing bribe or a debate he was trying to win, with me being the shiny prize. We skipped the honeymoon phase altogether and moved directly to a toxic and codependent situationship in a matter of months. And whatever his original reasons were for wanting to track my comings and goings (maybe trust?), he started abusing the app and turning it into his own personal playground, watching my every move. He often tricked me into thinking he was somewhere other than where he actually was, in order to make me jealous. One night he parked his car directly outside of STK, a restaurant where we often hung out, put on his blinkers, ran upstairs, ordered a soda, and sat at the bar to make it seem like he was having drinks with another woman. He was hoping I'd be checking up on him, which of course I was. His ruse got the reaction he was hoping for, and I immediately texted him saying "I thought you were staying home tonight?" After I accused him of cheating, he eventually came clean and admitted that his intent was just to upset me; for him it seemed jealousy equalled love. "I was in and out in about seven minutes, Karen. I'm sorry. It was really immature," he said. Another night when he said he was having a drink with a friend, he posted a picture to his Insta Story of him and a drop-dead gorgeous blond having what looked like a drink together. I immediately saw the post and tracked him to d|Bar. When I called him out on it, he came clean and let me know that she was just the DJ sitting at the table next to him on her break. It was at this moment that I realized my boyfriend was a 65-year- old *manchild* who was now playing dirty in the sandbox.

On another occasion, after returning home from an out-of-town visit, I called him up and asked if we could see each other. But after complaining that I didn't sound "enthusiastic" enough to him, he declined my invitation, saying that he was spending the night with his daughter. Feeling a little blown off, I ended up meeting a mutual guy friend of ours instead (admittedly someone he felt threatened by) in the lobby of the Shangri-La Hotel for drinks. After tracking my location and seeing exactly where I was, he jumped out of bed, quickly got dressed, and left his sleeping child in his condo alone to drive to STK at 1:00 a.m., making sure to send me a nasty text on the way. "I hope you and Max are having fun tonight; I'm out and about too," he messaged me. By now this sort of thing was happening quite often, and the whole keeping constant tabs on me (and vice versa) was damaging our relationship. What was cute at first was quickly becoming a very different beast.

Are You Sure You Want to Delete This Contact?

After breaking up and getting back together about a half dozen times over the course of a year, we were finally in somewhat of a healthy place where we were hanging out and having sex regularly. And although I hadn't given him back his "boyfriend" title just yet (he still needed to earn it), for all intents and purposes we were back together. So much so that we were about to hop on a plane for a mini vacay to South Beach. It was a final attempt at a fresh start for us, after a year of on-and-off dating. But a week before we were scheduled to leave, he let it slip that a woman he'd

As I said other than that obligation of a classical pianist for an hour and a half I don't plan on dating. You are a free agent, nothing I can do.

It's a date. You picked her up in a coffee shop and exchanged numbers. That's a date. She is not a friend bc you don't pick up "friends" in a coffee shop.

If you date I date

Delivered

Yes it was weeks ago...I'm not dating.. but I guess you're allowed your 1 date - all I know is how I feel.. I am not dating!

met at Starbucks while we were on one of our "Ross and Rachel" so-called breaks had invited him to the symphony. I expressed my disapproval, but quickly dropped it thinking there was no way he'd actually go on the date and jeopardize our relationship. But a few days later he mentioned it again, saying he was obligated to go because she had already purchased the seats. "There's no way you're going out on a date with another woman while we're together," I scoffed. He said nothing, but I wasn't convinced that he was going to respect my wishes (the fact that I didn't trust him should have been a clue that the relationship was doomed). What followed was certainly not my finest hour.

On the night of the symphony he was allegedly not attending, I called the box office to do some digging. What I found out was that HE was the one who purchased the tickets, not her, having ordered them online using his own name and credit card through his personal email account (so much for privacy protection right? The box office had no problem revealing the information when I told them I was his girlfriend). It was confirmed then—he was officially cheating on me and had lied to my face about taking another woman out. And this was five days before our scheduled vacation! Nice. Why he would risk it knowing I always had access to his location I will never understand. Later that same evening while having a martini with my friend Jax, I made one final check to confirm that he was, without a doubt, at the concert hall enjoying the symphony. The algorithm showed that he was indeed enjoying some harmony, though it certainly wasn't with me. Now I was officially done. Curtain closed. I immediately stopped sharing my location and deleted him and the app from my phone entirely. And since I wasn't about to forgo the trip to Florida that he and I had planned, I booked a revenge flight (think *Eat Pray Love*, but the opposite) to the same destination with one of my girlfriends instead. And although my whereabouts were now "unknown," you can be damn sure that I went. It was far too late to repair our relationship at this point; the damage was done. What started out as a cute way for us to stay in touch through GPS had ultimately led us to a completely different place, shutting us down and ending our communication for good. While I was done using the tracking app to monitor the location of my ex, I'm thankful it opened my eyes to the location our relationship was headed, which was clearly Nowheresville. Bye, boi.

Chapter 19

I've Never Seen Her Before In My Life

. . . .

U mmm, did my boyfriend just throw me under a godforsaken bus? On this night it was actually more of a vodka train, but the answer is yes. The 65-year-old I've mentioned only a few dozen times did just that. And for what? Let me unpack . . . About six months into our relationship, we were celebrating Valentine's Day at an upscale restaurant. Without thinking anything of it, I had playfully smuggled in a few harmless ounces of alcohol inside of my very fashionable and discreet Etsy flask bracelet. Do I regret doing it? Not really. I just hated getting caught. I will admit that the whole thing was stupid and childish on my part, and I probably could have left the arm candy at home. But there's a far bigger issue at play than me filling up a bracelet flask with vodka and then getting caught red-handed while topping up our drinks. Because if your man doesn't have your back—someone who's always supposed to love, support, defend, honour and protect you—he is definitely not the one.

Does a $950 Clic Clac H bracelet from Hermes, which I still love and wear to this day, look like the type of gift I'd get from a guy I just met? Someone taking me out for the very first time and on Valentine's Day of all nights? Well, that's exactly how my boyfriend painted it to the manager that evening when we, or more accurately me, got caught bootlegging in his establishment. And what started out as a gag gift that my sister and I bought each other to carry around in Vegas (where it's 100% legal to carry booze in public and also pretty much expected), quickly turned into *A Nightmare on 99 Yorkville Ave.*, at Italian restaurant Sofia, which ironically isn't too far from Elm Street.

Banned From Sofia Restaurant

This wasn't the first time my boyfriend had seen me pull a BYOD* at a high-end restaurant, or any one of my other shenanigans for that matter, which he'd always claimed was adorable. So why the outrage and upset on this particular date night? Well, clearly I had embarrassed him and I had made him look stupid in front of the swanky area's high society, which he considered himself to be part of based on the condo he had a block away. I do understand that gaining the approval of others is important and something we all seek. Social media continues to thrive because of this concept alone. So I get why he was so angry; I'd be hella mad too. But his reaction should have been motivated first and foremost by the desire to protect and defend me, his girlfriend, rather than maintaining appearances and

. . . .

* BYOD—Bring Your Own Drink.

gaining the respect and approval from a small group of people who were nowhere near our vicinity that night. Let me elaborate. . .

The matriarch of his fourth-generation fashion retailer family, AKA his very powerful, highly successful and extremely wealthy mother (what a joy!), scares the shit out of him no less today than she did when he was a little boy. To this day she still controls his portion of the family business, his inheritance, and his life. If word ever got out that he was dragging their prominent name (which is attached to a multi-designer Canadian boutique) through the mud, or doing something she didn't sign off on (like dating a woman 20 years his junior, or spending time with someone who smuggles vodka into an upscale restaurant in a cleverly crafted bracelet flask), he might be totally cut off. He'd been going along with almost everything his mother said for most of his life, always making sure to look respectable in the eyes of his family, his peers and the highly judgmental community we belong to so he could eventually cash in on his big windfall. Don't get me wrong, I too would adjust my behaviour and act accordingly if I was put in the same position. It's not uncommon or unreasonable to be influenced by a family member (or friend) when there's a significant amount of money at stake. Protecting a family legacy, even when there's no money involved, seems fair and justified. What I took issue with, though, was how he treated me in the process. A united front we definitely were not.

When the dick GM rushed over to our table threatening to call the cops because one of our dirty martini rounds happened to be *on me*, which I admit was in very *pour* taste but not a crime, my boyfriend should have handled things differently. We were regulars there, spending tons of cash on fancy dinners each week (well he did), and we were completely in love at this point. But instead of laughing it off as yet another one of his kooky girlfriend's antics and ordering apology shots for everyone including one for the owner

ing me to never wear the damn bracelet again, giving me the silent

who also happened to be there that night, he got up from the table to talk privately with an already livid manager, leaving me alone at my seat. "It's my first date with this broad, and she's clearly nuts. I'll never bring her here again. You have my word," I overheard him saying. "Are you fucking serious?" I whispered to him as the owner of the restaurant was walking over to our table. By now my buzz was killed, I was extremely embarrassed (mortified actually), and our romantic Valentine's Day celebration was clearly over. But he wouldn't leave, threw $100 bucks on the bar, and ordered another round.

A Bottle of Wine for Your Trouble, Sir

Is there no such thing as loyalty anymore? Because I can't imagine any scenario where I wouldn't have my man's back. But I'm also the idiot who stood by a guy who called a woman the C-word for not removing wet clothes from the dryer, remember? So rather than asking me to never wear the damn bracelet again, giving me the silent treatment (like a normal boyfriend would do!) or just letting it all go, he went back to the restaurant a few days later with another woman, hoping to present someone more impressive and respectable than me, and gifted the manager with a bottle of expensive wine. Sadly, this wasn't the first time he'd pretended to be out on a date with another woman. He often did this to piss me off or to make me jealous (unfortunately I had gotten used to his games). On this particular night, though, he chose to lie in order to save face. "You did what?" I yelled. "Karen, I love you, but I'm a [insert prestigious last name here] and have a reputation to uphold," he explained. "She's just a friend, I promise you. But I can't have anyone, especially my mother if this ever got back to her, thinking that I'm associated with someone like you." Wow. Just wow. I knew he was still mad and had every right to be (I'd already apologized and taken accountability for my misjudgement), but I didn't appreciate how he used it as an opportunity to downplay our relationship once again and appease his already disapproving family, on top of the wait staff and a manager he'd only met a few times. How he chose to handle the situation made me question whether he would ever have my back in the future. At this point, he wasn't the kind of boyfriend I wanted or certainly deserved. So, I reached for the bracelet flask I'd purposely forgotten to remove from my oversized LV, took a swig, and privately toasted the inevitable ending to this relationship. A dirty (martini) job, but someone had to do it.

Chapter 20

Herstory, History, or the Truth?

. . . .

I honestly never thought I'd get to where I am today, but here I stand! And after so many excruciating months, nine to be exact, I can finally say with complete certainty that I am over my ex. Yay for me! I finally see him for the lowlife that he is, when I was blind to it before. Phew. It seems like it took forever to clear the dust from clouding the truth of who and what he really is, but the dust did dissipate. If you're wondering how I ended up at this enlightened place after being so hung up on him for so long, let me explain the steps I took to get here, and of course spill the tea on how his DICK MOVES actually helped me move forward. It was most definitely a process, and a really hard one at that, but I did do it, and so can you.

My Healing Process: Try These Steps, They Work!

STEP 1: Wait

He will eventually do or say something after the breakup that will instantly change how you view or feel about him. Whether it's something big or small, I promise once this happens, you'll be done. It'll be your "Aha!" moment. Celebrate it. For me, it was a Facebook video clip that I saw him in on a mutual friend's page (a rare sighting since he used social media only to creep, not share) that turned me off. Just like that.

STEP 2: Question

Start questioning the past and examine all the events that foreshadowed and showcased the asshole that he is today. The signs were all there. You just overlooked or ignored them.

STEP 3: Remember

Think about that famous quote, "There are three sides to every story: your side, my side and the truth."

STEP 4: HERstory

Time to take a trip down memory lane. Visit your side of the story, reflect on the relationship and try to figure out what went wrong. Make a mental list of all the times he disappointed you, made you feel like shit, acted like a douche or treated you badly. Remembering those things will help you realize how much better you are without him.

STEP 5: HIStory

Do not try and make sense out of his side of the story. You won't. It's really just YOURSTORY anyway. HIStory is just your take on what you think happened.

STEP 6: Truth

This is the final step. Growth is accepting that he changed his mind, regardless of what the reasons were. They don't matter. Clearly something happened in his head to shift things. What it was is irrelevant at this point. Focus on moving forward instead. Why things ended have nothing to do with HERSTORY or HISTORY. The Truth is YOUR story. And your story has brought you to where you are today, accepting that the relationship was not meant to be. It's time to move on.

The Jump-Start to My Healing Process

Do I still think about him (TRIGGER WARNING) whenever I hear our song I.F.L.Y?* Of course I do. Still, thinking about him occasionally doesn't mean I'd say hi if we ran into each other (we live in the same area) where he buys his two packs of regular du MAURIER Signatures every day. Gross. And I wouldn't. After seeing a video of him winter tubing on a mutual friend's Facebook page the other day, I knew I was unequivocally done. And all it took was a measly 10 seconds. Because his obnoxious, high-pitched and piercing

. . . .

* I.F.L.Y—The song, I Fucking Love You, by Bazzi (which was our song).

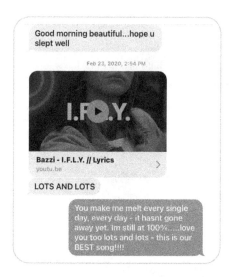

Good morning beautiful...hope u slept well

Feb 23, 2020, 2:54 PM

I.F.O.Y.

Bazzi - I.F.L.Y. // Lyrics
youtu.be

LOTS AND LOTS

You make me melt every single day, every day - it hasnt gone away yet. Im still at 100%.....love you too lots and lots - this is our BEST song!!!!

"WHASSUP???? I'm going to throw up," as he plunged down the snow hill at full speed made *me* sick. And the actual sound of his voice, which used to be the biggest turn-on, was now cringeworthy. WebMD has informed me that I'm not alone, and that there are millions of women out there who also suffer from Misophonia, or a strong dislike or hatred for specific irritating sounds, in this case disdain whenever our ex-boyfriends open their mouths! It is said, though, that what we're most attracted to at the beginning of a relationship often ends up being what we despise the most after it's over. The good news is that knowing I've moved on and am in a better place today means I can finally begin a new chapter, not only for this book, but more importantly in my life.

HERSTORY

48 Hours of Abuse Isn't So Bad, Said No One Ever

Have you ever been in a relationship with a guy who treated you like a punching bag . . . but only on Mondays and Tuesdays? Preposterous I know. But that's exactly what happened to me. It's Asshole Memory Number One, and the first of many instances that helped me heal and move on. Mondays and Tuesdays I was in the line of fire, but come hump day, we were doing just that, and he was again worshipping the ground I walked on. I didn't really notice the hot and cold behaviour so much until it became a regularly scheduled

occurrence. Should I have
been marking down the
dates in my Louis Vuitton
PM agenda every time he
was distant, cold, nasty or
mean, just like he'd been
doing with my bloody
periods? I didn't need to
because the weekly mis-
conduct happened like

> He's not playing games he's just being his usual self. All the same shit will always be there - no job, moody etc... we are just talking and taking things slow. I'm trying to figure out if I even want to be with him.
>
> Delivered

> Well it's Saturday so isn't this a good day....Ugly only happens Monday and Tuesday 😌. Look most people have no clue now.. maybe he should take the time and figure out what he wants. It's your journey Karen, do what makes your heart and soul happy.

clockwork. His bloody period of grouchiness (see what I did there?!) was only at the onset of a brand-new workweek, and it sadly became a running joke amongst my circle of friends. Once, on a Saturday night, while engaging in his favourite past-time of getting drunk, he agreed to come to Vegas with me after I mentioned my friend Jennifer's 40th birthday coming up and a Mariah Carey residency at Caesars Palace. But by Tuesday afternoon, he was bitchin' about the $650 Hotwire flight and hotel (which was a fucking steal, if you ask me, and pennies in comparison to the five grand "cheating's-okay-in-a-different-area-code" trips he boasted about having taken in the past). "I said you didn't have to accompany me to Mariah, remember?" I joked. But laughing was only permitted between Wednesday and Sunday, and it was currently Tuesday. Today he was angry and in no mood for mini-vacay talk. Turns out, he was just upset and stressed about his current unemployment situation and funds, or lack thereof. Even though he was spending whatever money I presume his mother and the government were giving him like he didn't have a worry in the world, apparently a cheap trip to Vegas with his girlfriend just wasn't in the cards (poker is another story altogether). It seems all his frustrations about the state of his life and financial situation were taken out on me weekly, though only on Mondays and Tuesdays. Once the weekend rolled around and things had gone back to normal, meaning he had started drinking his problems away, he was apologetic and seemed sincere and I was happy once again. That is, until it was time for bed on Sunday night. Then it was . . . Lather. Rinse. Repeat.

HISTORY
Or Just MYSTORY Continued?

I won't sit here and make excuses for his bad behaviour or offer possible reasons for why our relationship ended so abruptly. I can guess, but I can't know what he was thinking or why he did the things he did. All I know is that one day it seemed things were great between us, and the next day he wanted out. As my sister always reminds me, we all have the right to change our minds whenever we want, walk away, and move on to something bigger and better than a Sexypringle (gasp, is there even such a thing?!) without ever providing an explanation. We don't OWE anyone an explanation or even the courtesy of a goodbye, even if it's the right thing to do. Although an actual reason would have been nice to have, there's certainly no rule requiring it. And if I'm being honest, even without ever having been given a reason for his sudden change of heart, I can guess why it happened. He was just doing what he did best . . . cue the sabotage. Asshole Memory Number Two. When you spend most of your day feeling like a fraud or waiting for your partner to find out that you're not who you're pretending to be, beating us to the punch and reaching for a classic, cliché excuse is expected. Should I have listened when he initially warned me that he wasn't sure he was ready for a girlfriend? Of course. But the dude was 51 years old, not some high school student dealing with his first acne breakout and learning about love for the first time. It's hard to believe any man half a century old wouldn't be ready for a girlfriend. "Do you want to break up?" I insecurely asked him the first time he sprung the whole "I'm not in a great place in my life right now" garbage on me. "No, Kare. I love you. I just don't like being accountable to anyone; not my children and certainly not to you. It was bad enough when it was just me and the kids, but now I have another person to worry about. It's a lot," he explained. Asshole Memory Number Three. What the actual fuck? But he assured me we were fine and he promised to stop pulling away whenever he was feeling crappy, and I bought it, pushing aside the little voice warning me that a grown man supposedly in love was finding it too much to have to factor his children and a woman into his life. Wanna guess which day of the week this conversation took place on?

The Truth
What Triggered the Break-Up

To say there were defining moments that screamed "THE END IS NEAR" is an understatement. Although he'd probably emphatically maintain that our relationship had simply run its course and suffered a natural death, in reality there were very specific events that ultimately led to the death of us. The timing was impeccable, and the truth speaks for itself. Up until the very end, I thought we were mad-serious about each other and had a very real future together—we're talking, the last one standing at the final rose ceremony! He's the one who suggested walking down the aisle, after all. He used to jokingly tell me, "I started out with a KZ, and I'm gonna end up with a KZ." (His ex-wife and I share the same initials, and he liked to romanticize the irony of it all.) I believed him at first, but our "destined" future started to look pretty bleak not long after we visited his friend's house for brunch one Sunday afternoon. Had I known he was going to make a mockery of himself and get plastered that day, I would have feigned ill and bailed on the invitation. But I had no idea what was coming, so I played the good girlfriend, put on my magic skinny jeans, curled my long black hair (correction, my $1000 extensions), and I joined him for an afternoon in the 'burbs with new friends. When he started pounding back the scotch, slurring his words, and getting louder with each shot, I discreetly suggested that he might want to pace himself. Then the frequent visits to the powder room, no pun intended, started. Every time he left me alone at the table to go outside for a smoke, someone would ask me if I was okay, assuring me that this was how he always behaved at gatherings, and that I shouldn't take it personally (if only he were as considerate to me as his friends were). By now he was incoherent and wobbly on his feet, but claiming he was okay to drive. The car ride home, with me in the driver's seat, was not a pleasant one. While he struggled to stay awake between hiccups, fumbling through his Apple Music playlist for Tyga's *Taste*, and declaring his undying love for me, I tried to make some sense of his behaviour. I had been aware that he had a drinking problem, but I hadn't realized how serious it was until I witnessed it in broad daylight. When I called later to say that I didn't want to be tied to an alcoholic and that this was a deal-breaker for me, he minimized my worries and concerns and promised to tone it down. My warning that day seemed to have scared him into thinking I was about to throw in the towel, so three days later he took his final shot with me (Asshole Memory Number Four) and beat me to the punch.

Our Last Day as Boyfriend and Girlfriend

Immediately following the Sunday brunch fiasco, things appeared to be okay. I had moved on from the incident, thinking our discussion afterwards meant he'd tone down the alcohol and the antics moving forward. Monday and Tuesday he was unapproachable, as expected, but my plan was to rock his world on Wednesday. I invited him over for some mid-day play, hoping for an afternoon of naked fun. When he arrived in his Corona inspired attire (sweats and a hoodie), I was knee-deep in work; I was the one with the actual job, remember. So he sat patiently on my couch waiting for his boss bitch to wrap things up. Here was my boyfriend sitting in a house that I own (he rents), watching me work from home (when he has no job or future prospects), aimlessly scrolling through his phone, waiting

to get his dick wet. Emasculating much? When I was finally ready to go, I immediately jumped on top of him, pulled down his oversized Walmart joggers, and playfully asked what we were doing that night. "I might go up north to a friend's cottage" he casually said, but dem were fighting words and he knew it. Asshole Memory Number Five. "I thought Wednesdays were ours?" I reminded him, confused by this sudden change in what had always been our weekly date night. Looking back, I believe my reaction to the previous weekend's brunch incident had likely already prompted him to start planning his exit strategy, so this was the perfect excuse to create a fight and storm out, which is exactly what he did. WTF? "Don't leave," I texted after he was already out the door, but he didn't respond or even turn around. Asshole Memory Number Six. Later that night he didn't utter a word about how he'd abruptly left my place, pretending everything between us was fine. When I got frustrated with his inability to address what had just happened and texted him saying "I am so done right now," he replied back in agreement. Asshole Memory Number Seven. The next day he called it quits for good. In hindsight, this sudden breakup three days after that dreadful drunken episode at his friend's place was inevitable. If I had kept quiet or looked the other way every time he got wasted and acted like a buffoon, would things have been different? Maybe for a short while. Triggers only bring to the surface what's been there all along. Had it not been this, it would have been something else. But it will always end up being something. He was right about one thing, though; until you find peace, get your shit together and clean up your act, perhaps even earn that sobriety chip, Sexypringles are never long-term options. They're fun for a while, but impossible to maintain and hold on to. The truth hurts, right? And although it took me forever and a day to come to this realization, I'm here now and I'm damn proud of it.

Chapter 21

Don't Worry,
I'm Not that Karen

ave I ever been called a Karen pejoratively, or been accused
of perpetuating the infamous Karen Meme? Nope. Not once.
At least not to my knowledge. But there may have been an incident
a few years back involving the Vice President of the Colosseum in
Las Vegas, that would put any real, white, middle-aged Karen, likely
born in the 1970s, to shame. I may have sent an email and then hella
escalated a situation when it didn't go my way. Which I suppose
kind of makes me THAT Karen. But in my defence . . . it had nothing
to do with race, privilege, or even a short haircut, and almost everything to do with Queen Mariah Carey. For those of you who don't
know me well, my obsessive personality stretches far beyond gently
stalking ex-boyfriends—celebrities and musicians have always been

fair game too! And although I've never waited outside Mariah's New York City penthouse like my very first Lambily friend Sergio did, I've been a loyal fan of Mimi's practically my whole life. So, when she signed a two-year Las Vegas residency deal at Caesars Palace in Las Vegas, I was excited for the opportunity to see my idol in such an intimate venue, and in a city I visit so often that I consider it to be my second home (TRUE STORY: I've entered Nevada enough times over the years that U.S. Customs Officials once accused me of being a drug mule). I'm lucky enough to have seen Mariah multiple times, at multiple locations, and I consider myself to be a hardcore and loyal AF fan. My loyalty has even allowed me to enjoy some VIP perks. One night the Colosseum security staff, who all knew me, let me remain in an empty front row center seat I'd snuck into instead of escorting me back to the third-row seat I'd purchased. The amazing outcome of sitting this close? Mariah spoke directly to me for a few minutes, and even posed for a pic, saving me $1,000 US for the meet-and-greet package I wanted to purchase like my lamb friends Claire, Justin and Jennifer did! I was also close enough that night to inappropriately, though inadvertently, gently caress Mimi's arm when she walked past me (hands-down, she has the softest skin I've ever touched. I hear she bathes in buttermilk). I almost got kicked out, but it was so worth it! What I think is clear at this point is that I'm not just any fan . . . I'm one of THOSE fans.

What Do You Meme the Answer is No?

After scoring a second-row ticket for a Mariah Carey concert back in the summer of 2016, I thought it might be fun to bring my son along with me. He was around six years old, so it was time to finally introduce him to one of his mom's idols. But I didn't want to give up my hard-to-acquire and awesome single second-row BB-407 seat;

plus, I had this delusional "Sweet, Sweet Fantasy, Baby" that Mariah might take notice of the adorable mom-and-son duo in the audience and call him up on stage, so I contacted the Colosseum directly to see if he could sit on my lap during the concert. Not surprisingly, they said no, and although I appreciated the personal reply from the VP himself, I wasn't willing to accept his dismissive "it's company policy" excuse without at least a little bit of a fight. So when Bret, the Manager assigned to my complaint, called me back to discuss my issue further, it was game on! "People sitting behind you will complain," he said, to which I argued that "everyone stands anyway, so a little kid sitting on my lap won't offend anyone." Still, he wouldn't budge and so I gave up, left my son at home, flew to Vegas alone and attended the concert solo.

But on the night of the concert when I turned around and saw a couple with their two grown-ass children sitting on each of their parents' laps, without security addressing the situation or the slightest peep from anyone around us, I tried not to lose my shit. It was hard, though. I asked the couple how they were able to get past security without tickets for their children. "Well, it's all about who you know, right?" the woman said. At this point it wasn't that I felt any sense of entitlement, as my name has come to suggest nowadays, but rather, I just wanted to be treated the same as everyone else, particularly like this very lucky couple. So, when I got back to Toronto I turned into THAT Karen and immediately called the head office demanding to speak to "the manager," Bret.

Am I Really that Karen?

If you Google Karen Meme characteristics, you get (1) rude to service workers, (2) a sense of entitlement, (3) white privilege, (4) believes she's right even when she's wrong, and (5) speaks to the manager.

Two out of five ain't bad! But seriously, I promise I'm not that Karen! Did the President and CEO of Liberty Entertainment Group and owner of BlueBlood Steakhouse hold an emergency staff meeting after I complained about the lack of blue cheese olives one night? Yes. But I'd only casually complained to the manager Geoff, who also happens to be my friend, that they were out of them once, and it was Geoff who let it slip. Is someone in the basement of Casa Loma as we speak stuffing olives with blue cheese, because my name came up on their reservation list today? Most likely. Am I the girl who hates getting charged an extra $3 for guacamole at Chipotle, or gets a little *meshuga* if I'm not handed a coffee sleeve at Tim's? Yes. Do I bite my tongue at the movies if I can't get an extra popcorn bag to portion some out for my son? Another yes. But I'm still not that Karen! I practise using my "inside voice" and keep all these pent-up feelings to myself, only to unleash them later when I bitch about them to my mom.

After leaving several aggressive voicemails to Bret with no response, he finally called back. "Remember that company policy bullshit and the 'I'm sorry there are no exceptions' email you sent?" I pointed out. But before he had a chance to respond, I proceeded to tell him about the family I'd witnessed getting preferential treatment over me. "I will speak to my security staff and look into it," he said. But this wasn't quite good enough, and my namesake came out in full force. "Comp two front-row tickets for me and my son, to any upcoming show, and this will all go away," I said. "What?" he laughed and immediately hung up. When we finally connected again after I continued to blow up his phone with message after message, he threatened to charge me with harassment. At this point, everyone on his management team, along with the rest of his staff, knew my name. "I swear I'm a nice girl and not a stalker!" I tried apologizing for taking things too far, but I'd finally broken him. "What are the dates you're looking for?" he asked. "I will call you back and let you know if someone will sign-off on your request." An hour later he offered me a front-row ticket but said he couldn't get clearance to comp me a seat for my son. I happily accepted his offer and apologized again, more profusely this time, offering to take him out for a "thank-you" martini before the upcoming show. "We are going to be good friends," I joked. He politely declined my offer and quickly ended the call.

Oh Shit, Maybe I Really Am that Karen

On the night of the concert, I was still determined to meet Bret and take him out for that drink. I truly believed that once he saw how sexy I was in person, instead of the overweight, middle-aged, Abby Lee Miller reality star from *Dance Moms* that I'm sure he envisioned me looking like, he would actually want to hang out. I bugged him a few more times, but he kept saying he was too busy to meet. When I arrived early at Caesars Palace on the night of the concert and asked someone at the box office to grab Bret, it went exactly as predicted. The minute he walked out to greet me, the angry and annoyed man who was forced to give me a front-row seat, and who initially wanted absolutely nothing to do with me, was suddenly singing a very different tune. "Hey, we can grab that martini now if you want and then I'll personally escort you to your seat" he said, as we walked across the casino floor to the Vista Cocktail Lounge. He was quick to mention that the tight black leather pants I was wearing looked fantastic. Just like that, we were good, and I was magically no longer THAT Karen anymore. And from that night forward, whenever I went to see Mariah at Caesars, Bret always reserved me a front-row seat. Today, even though so many years have passed, and he no longer works at the Colosseum, things still ended on a high note (we're talking the glass-breaking pitches that only MC can hit) and we remain friendly. But shit, although I was and still am obsessed with Mariah, and I blame her entirely for my behaviour, I guess I really am THAT Karen after all.

Chapter 22

Kiss and Tell

. . . .

As little girls, we go from dreaming about our first kiss to imagining who's going to be our last, patiently waiting for our search to be over. And although it's sometimes hard for men to be vulnerable, open up and reveal their true feelings and intentions, the way they kiss can literally speak volumes. Kissing is far more revelatory than many of us think. The act of two pairs of lips joining together is actually one of the most intimate acts of affection there are, and it's hands down the best part of meeting someone new. So how do you know if he's really interested? That's easy. His lips will tell you everything you need to know, without ever saying a word.

Have I kissed a ton of frogs in my lifetime, and occasionally succumbed to those fairy-tale fallacies we've all been bombarded with since birth? Yes. Thanks Walt. But I'm also proud to say that I haven't been sitting around waiting to be saved either. Because I've been slaying it all on my own and doing just fine, thank you very much. But truth be told, I'd trade it all in a heartbeat for those damn butterflies. When I look back at all the men (and women) I've kissed, I really have no complaints. My first kiss with Jamie at Camp Robin Hood when I was 13 years old is one of my sweetest archived childhood memories. Mainly because we are still friends today, but also because it was a monumental "first" for us both. But since then, it's been a sort of mix between Vanilla and Neapolitan. As mentioned, I stayed with a man for over a year who kissed me like a G-ddamn woodpecker. Although we adapted as best we could (or I should say, I adapted), it's not my fondest memory. I've also had a bunch of mediocre relationships that at the time felt packed with passion but in retrospect I now realize lacked any real chemistry. Thankfully I've also had a few real-life movie moments too; we're talking earth shattering and unrestrained, à la *The Notebook*. And once that happens, there's just no turning back. Meaning, we should never settle for anything less than fireworks.

Will the Guy You're Currently Kissing Make It to the Finish Line?

Ask Yourself These Questions Cosmo May Have Missed!

☐ **Was He Shy at The Beginning of The Relationship?**

If the extrovert you're dating who's normally the life of the party gets super shy and acts differently around you, this is a good thing. It is an indication of genuine care and interest. When a man is nervous, it means he's got something to lose, and he will likely be on his best behaviour, trying hard to impress you until he knows you're 100% in. The intent is there. So, let's see where things go.

☐ Do You Spend Hours JUST Kissing?

Intimacy is super important in a relationship, and kissing is one of the best ways to form a more meaningful connection. So, if you notice yourself reverting to those innocent adolescent days of hours long kissing sessions (foggy car windows included!), this is a good sign. Oh, and if your face is raw and scratched up from his scruff after you're done, you're both crazy about each other!

☐ Can You See Into Each Other's Soul?

Allowing yourself to be vulnerable in front of someone is key to a lasting relationship. It's about taking a risk and really trusting your partner on a deeper level. If he's not afraid to show emotion and truly be seen by you, and he's able to express how he feels, this means he's comfortable with you and trusts you wholeheartedly. If he makes love to you doggie-style every single time, and there's never any eye contact (even when you're on top), you're probably not quite there yet.

☐ Did You Wait to Have Sex?

This is hands down, my new favourite jam (although I haven't always practiced what I'm now preaching). If you can both hold off, trust me, it's so much better in the end. Plus, you're creating a better foundation for an endless romance. In my experience, the relationships where I've exercised restraint rather than jumping in headfirst have always served me best. Men who are patient and wait (instead of buying into the expectation of sex after only three dates) usually are more invested in developing a long-term, committed relationship. When the physical stuff comes after a meaningful connection has been established, the build-up and delay is always damn well worth it. Trust me on this one.

☐ Is He Your Partner in Crime?

If he's helped you sneak mini strawberry jam jars (not marmalade) into your purse from your favourite restaurant, you may have found your Clyde. Whatever it is you're secretly into, for a relationship to work you both need to be on the same page. This is key. If you can break the law with your partner, and not get caught of course, you're off to a good start. In my *book*(s) anyway!

☐ Can You Reveal Your Flaws Without Judgement?

We've all got bags of shit that we don't want, and helping each other unpack them suggests unconditional love. Be careful, though; sometimes you end up with baggage you don't want or need, with a ton of heavy lifting required.

☐ Does He Grab Your Face with Both Hands When He Kisses You?

Every girl's dream, no matter what your age, and the ultimate goal. Right?

☐ Is He Tender with You? Does He Give You Forehead Kisses?

It's so not dismissive! Rather, it's a compassionate, non-sexual way to communicate adoration and respect. Studies have shown that forehead kisses are a sign of deep affection and that men who kiss us on our foreheads are completely smitten and in love!

☐ Do You Have Your Own Language of Love?

Do you share a ton of private inside jokes and/or special words or phrases that go beyond just adorable pet names? (Naming our sweet spot *Cleopatra* doesn't count!). If so, you've got an unbreakable bond that's timeless and worth the same as gold.

☐ Are You Nervous When You're Around Each Other?

Do you still get butterflies and sweaty palms even after six months? Do days apart feel like forever? (For me, when the nausea hits, I'm usually falling in love.) Are you way too excited to see him on your regularly scheduled date night? Does it always feel like the first time? If so, this probably isn't going away any time soon.

☐ Do You Share Secrets?

Do you confide in each other about all the private and sacred stuff (not just the little things our gal pals tell us in confidence that we let slip during pillow talk but all the more personal bits)? If so, you've got the makings of a lasting relationship. If he's sharing too, opening up and trusting you with all of his secrets, including the one where he caught his mom cheating, this is a good sign. A man who lets you in and reveals the confidential shit is probably bringing you home to meet his parents. All you need to do now is put your game face on and pretend you know nothing about the infidelity! Clearly, you've got an unbreakable bond based on loyalty and trust. Take it.

Bonus Tip for Men

When a woman tells you she doesn't KISS on a first date, she's lying. We all do!

1 To 2 ✓: Kiss Him Goodbye—Consider this one just practice. Spin the Bottle again to see who's next.

3 To 5 ✓: Shut Up And Kiss Me—The honeymoon phase isn't ending anytime soon, neither are those Seven Minutes in Heaven.

6+ ✓: Sealed With A Kiss—Clearly, you're both in it to win it. Grab a deck of cards, it's time to play Suck and Blow.

If you've checked off most of this list, you may be approaching your last kiss. Trust it. On a side note, my first kiss Jamie is happily married to a wonderful woman and off the market! But good and genuine guys are out there, waiting. So, let's go find them and interrupt their lives! Your new journey begins now. I know mine has. It's all about finding someone who appreciates your worth, who doesn't take you for granted and, of course, who KISSES you like nobody else's business. Who's with me?

Chapter 23

Life According to Carrie Bradshaw

Anyone who knows me well will understand why this particular chapter needs no introduction. None at all. Why, you ask? Because I'm fully obsessed with *Sex and the City* (have been for years) and consider myself to be a real-life Carrie Bradshaw. Heck, my life's so extra that a spin-off based on my own mishaps could be Candace Bushnell's next syndicated hit! Every episode of *SATC* is all about us girls, right? And whether you identify with Samantha, Charlotte, Miranda, or Carrie (we all want to be Carrie, though), there are so many things we can learn from the entire DVD boxset (a COVID purchase). So which lessons should we dive into? As I re-watch every season in its entirety thanks to the pandemic, umm, without a doubt the answer is . . . all of them! Let's explore.

The Sex on The First Date Curse

"I was dying to sleep with him. But isn't delayed gratification the definition of maturity?"

—CARRIE

Going back and restarting a series from the beginning is like eating a chocolate éclair when you haven't touched one in years and then remembering just how fabulous it actually tastes. Now, thanks to the pandemic, an increase in eating, and my new 75" Samsung Frame TV, I'm regularly indulging in both!

Rewatching Big and Carrie's first encounters, before their six-plus years of drama that followed, reminds me of some of my own past loves. All that back and forth, the never knowing where we stand, the intense roller coaster ride; you get the idea. But when it comes to sex, I wonder: *Is There Such a Thing As Too Soon?* I certainly used to think so, but now I'm not so sure. Just the other night when I was weighing in on a "should I hook up with this chick I just met on Tinder?" convo with my friend Dave, this very topic came up. And as I built my case for why waiting is better than jumping right in (on top of a real fear of catching COVID), I realized my theory might have some cracks. Because there have been men who I've waited to sleep with that bailed after just a few months (specifically my most recent ex), and others I gave it up to right away who ended up committing for years. So why was Carrie so worried that she'd had sex with Big too soon? In the end, they did get married after all, so did it really matter WHEN it happened? Lesson One: When it comes to having sex early on, research has shown that the timing of first-time sex doesn't predict how good the relationship will be or how long it will last. The more important things, like connection, chemistry, interest, and intent, ultimately determine how things will go. The evidence speaks for itself. In the end, my friend Dave decided not to wait and just go for it, and I'm happy to report that it went well for him. I still say fuck it, though not literally. I'm Team Aidan when he tells Carrie "let's wait." Because my story ends with someone just like him. And luckily for me, he's right around the corner, patiently anticipating my arrival. Now I just need to find that corner . . .

The Drought

"Jesus, Carrie come on, will you knock it the fuck off, I'm trying to watch the fight"

—MR. BIG

Thankfully, none of my sports-obsessed boyfriends have ever chosen to watch a game over having sex with me. So, what the heck was Big thinking? I guess like any new relationship, after a few months pass, the initial honeymoon phase passes too, and routines begin to form. As things get less new and we become more comfortable with each other, sex and spontaneity can change. When I observed Carrie and Big's sex life begin to decline on screen, I started to wonder: *Does Not Having Sex Regularly Mean Anything?* In Carrie's situation it didn't mean a thing, though she wasted so many brunches and mimosas stressing about it (are mimosas ever a waste though?!). When I was 22 and in love for the very first time, I found myself worried about this exact situation. Things were serious between my actor boyfriend and me at the time, and he was great. So great, in fact, that I moved to New Zealand with him for a few months when his work took him there. But this otherwise great guy didn't seem to enjoy sex, because we were hardly ever having it. And after spending months internalizing my feelings of rejection and thinking the problem was me, I finally summoned up the courage to say something. It turned out he was on medication to deal with a parasite he'd contracted a year prior while in Africa, when he ate crocodile poo after being dared to, while hosting Season Two of Nickelodeon's *Wild Side* (I can't make this (crocodile) shit up, people). As a result of the medication, his sex drive was nil. Lesson Two: Communication should be our biggest turn on. Talk is often the fix. Plus, addressing concerns upfront may prevent insecurities from spilling over into future relationships. I should have voiced my concerns sooner, but he also should have been more honest and upfront about what was going on (as embarrassing as that might have been for him). So find yourself a guy who knows how to properly communicate, and then try talking for a change.

Big Secrets

"I lied, I don't have to work, I'm meeting Big for lunch, and I didn't think you'd approve"

—CARRIE

Could our girlfriends be influencing our decisions and sabotaging our relationships without even knowing it? After Carrie breaks up with Big, she leans on Samantha, Charlotte and Miranda for support. But was she being persuaded by their opinions without even knowing it? "Wake up Carrie, how many more times are you going to go through this? He is bad for you," Miranda says, after Carrie reveals that she's talking to him again. Since everyone comes to the table with their own personal life experience, all judgments, even ones delicately wrapped in good intentions, are full of biases. So, I started to wonder: *When it Comes to Matters of The Heart, Are We Listening to Our Friends Instead of Trusting Our Own Instincts or Finding Things Out for Ourselves?* I'll admit that I am guilty of allowing my friends' opinions and harsh judgements to get the better of me, and then sabotaging my relationships with men solely based on what they've said. It's no surprise that Carrie chose not to tell anyone when she started sleeping with Big again; she didn't want the lectures. I also chose to keep quiet when I got back together with my ex last spring.

After I finally broke my silence and decided to tell everyone about our relationship, no one approved. Not a single soul. Here's what I've learned when it comes to letting our friends weigh in on relationships with toxic men. When two people are in love, their connection is a unique and private experience. Everyone else is an outsider. In Season Three, when Steve told Miranda right after getting back together that "only you and I can ever really know what happened between you and I. It's nobody else's business," this really resonated with me. Sometimes we just need to find out (on our own) if a relationship is going to work out or not. Experiencing pain is a lesson learned so we don't repeat the same mistakes again. But if we ASK for an opinion, we also shouldn't kill the messenger if we hear something we aren't ready to accept. When my ex and I got back together, we collectively made the decision not to take any advice from our friends and keep things strictly between us, because we knew how things looked. We wanted to give our second go-around a fair chance, without any disapproval, extra noise or unwanted stress; we already knew no one supported our reconciliation. Clearly we didn't work out in the end and our friends' instincts turned out to be right, but it was something we needed to find out for ourselves. Lesson Three: It's always a good idea to take into consideration what your friends are saying. Although your friends are seeing things through a different lens, they usually have your best interests at heart. If you ask, then LISTEN. If you're not ready to hear the truth, don't involve them in the process. In the end, it's your life, your happiness, and who you choose to wake up next to that matters most. Still, we sometimes need a little nudge from these bystanders to help lead us in the right direction.

Surprise! He's Back

"Jesus, well, I miss you. I can't fucking stop thinking about you.
There you have it"

—MR. BIG

When my good friend Sherri heard I was rewatching Season Three researching for this chapter, she got really excited. "This is the best season, Kare, you just wait," she excitedly informed me. And when Big shows up at Carrie's door unannounced, telling her he can't stop thinking about her, I finally understood what she meant. Because we're all just waiting for that grand gesture from the one we love, right? Does this turn us into "pathetic, needy, insecure victims who keep going back for more?" Carrie asks, after taking John back. I'm guessing she didn't learn the first time around that he was never going to change. So, I wondered: *When It Comes to Relationships, Should We Accept the Grand Gestures Following a Fuck-Up or Dismiss Them and Move On?* My opinion seems to depend on a few things, like which side of the bed I wake up on, or if I happen to be on the rag or not. Some days I'm hoping (and praying) that my ex will realize his mistake and show up at my door drunk at 1 a.m. (a modern-day grand gesture) or chase me down at the airport to stop me from flying to Vegas (a blockbuster movie grand gesture). I'm keeping it real, though; I'm a sucker for *any* declaration of love. Other days I want to try a different Jimmy (Choo) altogether, cut my losses and not accept any gesture, no matter how grand. Perhaps Carrie was onto something when she says that maybe we obsess over them and repeatedly take 'em back (even after the tiniest monumental act) because the relationship feels unfinished. Lesson Four: A grand gesture won't change who he is, how horribly he treated you, nor does it erase any of the reasons why you aren't together anymore. We need to stop obsessing over these guys—regardless of how many dozen roses they show up with (flowers die too, remember). Find someone who's never been in a position that warrants a grand gesture—a guy who isn't going to feed you a bunch of lies, or stage something big (or small) every time he fucks up. The goal is to find a guy who doesn't fuck up in the first place. *And Just Like That* . . . I'm still single.

Chapter 24

Life According to Carrie Bradshaw, the Ex-Files

· · · · · · · · · · · ·

L ast night I finished the remaining episodes of *Sex and The City*. So what the F-ing-Martini am I going to do now? Look into my own life and hope for my own *Carrie-Tale* ending? Because John came back. He actually came back. But the real life Bigs never do, right? They don't fly to Paris to seal the deal after six long seasons. The Mr. Prestons of my world can't afford that. But we continue to watch. Why? Because—dramatic pause—we all want to believe that true love exists, no matter how many tries it takes to get there. So, if you're a repeat offender like Carrie, and you still haven't gotten it right, strap on your Manolos and let's revisit that ex you just can't seem to shake. Class is now in session.

The "Getting Back with the EX" Dilemma

I'm a firm believer in second chances, and sometimes third and fourth ones too, if he's worth it. But it's rarely ever about the guy, and more often about chasing what you thought you once had, or the fantasy we see on TV. In Carrie's case, her attempts at getting back together with Big after countless breakups were never quite successful, but she kept running back for more. For me, whenever they've come back around (and they always do), it's never worked out. Carrie and Big did end up getting married, but this still got me thinking . . . *Is There a Secret to Making a Second, or Third, or Fourth Chance Work?* Actually, no. All it takes is a commitment from both parties involved and a shit ton of work, assuming it's something you BOTH want. Did you know that over 50% of couples break up and get back together, more than once? Ask Siri if you don't believe me.

If your ex was a Richard before things
went south, stop reading this chapter.
(These tips only apply to good guys.)

---

*Want It to Abso-fucking-lutely
Work Out this Time?*

Here's What To Do:

Stop Punishing Her for Big Mistakes

Although Aidan agrees to get back together with Carrie after she
cheats, his words never quite match his actions. Instead, he's mean,
unaffectionate and indifferent, which she notices right away. Do I get
that he was scared to trust her again and needed time to process the
betrayal? Sure. Do I get that he was still hurt and hadn't gotten over
those feelings yet? Yep. But why make her suffer if he truly wanted
her back? Yes, reconciliation can be messy and complicated. And
sometimes there's just too much anger and resentment (especially
around infidelity) to get past things, and it's not for lack of trying. But
Aidan went out of his way to hurt Carrie, trying to make her pay for
her mistake, and he got downright nasty, which wasn't fair either,
since he'd already agreed to the second attempt at fixing things.

TIP #1: *Give It Your All*

If you've agreed to give things another shot, then let the bullshit go,
or at least put in some effort and try. Because we notice when you're
being passive aggressive, even when it's subtle. It just makes us question the reconciliation and reach for triple vodkas instead (true story,

in my case). So, what's the alternative? Commit and follow through, and wait longer than a nano-second before calling it. If you aren't willing to put in the real work to try and get past things, why bother trying in the first place? Both parties need to be present and willing to try (the one at fault will need to try harder, obvs). Take responsibility for your actions and the role you played. Healing can happen; it IS possible (though not in every case). Be realistic. Research has shown that many couples do in fact get past things and move forward after breaking up; 50% to be exact, although this number drops drastically if an infidelity occurred, with only 16% of couples surviving an affair. While it's not always the case, it IS possible to build back the trust with some patience and a shit ton of effort. Only time will tell if the pieces can be put back together or not. Results will vary.

Change Old Behaviours

If the definition of insanity is doing the same thing over and over again and expecting a different result, then getting back with an ex without making any changes is downright crazy. Case in point, when Carrie runs back to Big after he has heart surgery. While Big promises to treat her differently this time, he's back to his old tricks the very next morning. This, in a nutshell, is nuts.

"It was a shift imperceivable to anyone but me, but I knew his heart had closed up again"

—CARRIE

TIP #2: *Confront Past Issues*

Any problems or issues you had previously must be addressed and dealt with before a successful reconciliation can take place. More importantly, your behaviour and the way you treat your partner needs to change (if he's an ASSHOLE in general, I've got nothing). When an ex I'd been dating for under a year suggested couples counselling, I agreed to go even though I secretly thought it was ridiculous—at this point the relationship, IMO, was already way too toxic and complicated to fix. But at least he was trying, and he suggested counselling, which was something completely different from how we'd been handling things in the past. I appreciated his proactive attempt. And although the doctor flat out told us after our first session that we had no chance in hell of surviving (was he even allowed to say this?), the experience still taught me a valuable lesson. Switching things up, getting help, or trying something new, instead of falling back into old patterns of behaviour, definitely ups the ante and increases your chances for success.

"We broke up one week after that appointment"

—SEXYPRINGLE

Let Go & Forgive. Then Start a New Relationship

After Steve reveals his one-time indiscretion, Miranda kicks him out and begins life as a single mom. But they still love each other and want to make things work. So how can we protect ourselves from getting hurt again if we decide to revisit our past? Well, we can't. "All you know is that you want to move forward and risk that the love that you have for each other won't allow that to happen again," Steve and Miranda's therapist tells them. The real work starts once you begin trying to get past the hurt, anger and betrayal.

TIP #3: *Be an Adult, Not a Child*

If you've been playing the victim, be accountable instead. We all fuck up, but it's how we choose to deal with it that separates the kids from the grownups. If you're both willing to acknowledge each other's mistakes, without continuously bringing it up and placing blame, the relationship can move forward. So, take a step back to think about the relationship, and take some time apart, too, to decide if getting back together is what you really want. Then meet up on the Brooklyn Bridge as Miranda and Steve do—or somewhere more local like STK in Yorkville. Because by showing up, you're making a promise to each other that you're willing to let it all go and move forward, as Miranda says. If the relationship is worth fighting for and your love is still salvageable, the $25 cocktails and mini wagyu burgers will be well worth it!

BONUS TIP: *Never Go Back to a Berger*

Take it from me, ladies . . . if he breaks up with you via a Post-It Note like Berger did to Carrie ("I'm sorry I can't, don't hate me"), or calls you on his way back from a pool party he didn't invite you to and says sayonara just a few days after your (*Punk'd*) birthday celebration or decides to bail on you without any warning or explanation, there really isn't much left to work with. Trust me. So, sleep well tonight sans all those crickets from that ridiculous noise-cancelling machine Berger couldn't sleep without, knowing that this time, instead of a sticky-note saying that HE can't, you're turning the tables and making the choice that YOU can't.

Chapter 25

Fuck, Marry, Kill

. . . .

Have you ever heard of the game KISS, MARRY, KILL, where you take any three people—they can be friends, celebrities, or even ex-boyfriends—and slot them into one of these three categories? For example, thanks to the pandemic I just finished re-watching the entire six seasons of *Prison Break* (immediately following *Sex and the City* of course). Round One: Lincoln Burrows (Dominic Purcell) is a definite KISS (AKA FUCK) situation. Have you seen his biceps?! Next up is Alexander Mahone (William Fichtner), who I'd MARRY in a heartbeat. In case you're at all interested in knowing my type, he's most definitely it. And lastly there's Theodore "T-Bag" Bagwell (Robert Knepper) who gets the KILL, since pedophiles belong deep in the ground. For Round Two: I've added a twist and have decided that my answers won't be based on just "fantasy" looks or sex appeal like they usually are. Instead, I'm going with real people; ex-boyfriends or guys I've briefly dated in the past, with the new categories, DISS, MARRY, KILL. Since I actually know these men in real life, I'll choose their title based on my overall opinion of them, combining all the things we use to make overall judgements about someone.

First Up: The Kill Spot

A few months back while trolling for guys on Facebook (yes, I sometimes use Facebook and Instagram as an alternative to eHarmony, Plenty of Fish or OKCupid to meet men), I accidentally met someone who happened to be friends with my ex-boyfriend. My first thought was HELL NO, but after some back-and-forth flirting he assured me that they didn't know each other well, and that he was nothing like my "loser" ex (his words). I believed him. The beautiful house he claimed to live in ended up being a friend's basement (a buddy going through a divorce who wanted the company). His black Pontiac convertible, belonged to his father. That Life Coach job he boasted about (after quitting his 9 to 5 to start his own "business") was just a babysitting gig for ASD and special needs kids—clients he stole from his psychotherapist ex-girlfriend who I heard employed him (and provided a roof over his head) back when they were together. Aside from the periodic bike rides and camping trips he took them on (at an hourly rate of course), his days were spent lounging by the backyard pool of his host friend, growing (and smoking) weed, and sending me shirtless selfies and never-ending texts. I also found out from a friend of mine that he had used her OHIP number to get reimbursed by the government for massages he had never paid for or even received (I'm guessing he was only interested in the ones that included a *Happy Ending*, like my ex-boyfriend!). One night, while we were driving home from dinner, he mentioned that my ex had signed up for AdultFriendFinder.com and fucked seven different women all in the span of a week. "How do you know this?," I asked. "He told me when we were at a friend's cottage in Wasaga a few months back," he replied. *So much for we rarely ever hang out,* I thought. The next day I decided to check out the sex site for myself. I'll admit I was curious and wanted to see if I'd be able to recognize my ex's dick, and then confirm everything I'd been told. But rather than finding my ex on the site, this guy I'd already gone out with a few times was exposed instead—his face though, not his junk. And it only took 500 words or less for me to discover that Mr. Pleasure69, was a real-life *Christian Grey*, a swinger looking for some role-play and NSA fun with like-minded women, and/or couples. He'd been an exclusive GOLD member for over a year. Holy fucking shit. Welcome to dating in 2021—where do I sign up? Why he had mentioned this site to me in the first place, knowing it might blow his cover, I will never understand. It was confirmed: I was dating a carbon copy of my ex. Actually, he was worse since I never did find proof that my ex was even on the site (despite my desperate search). For this incident alone—although there are so many other reasons why he deserves to perish in this game—he's now been BLOCKED and gets the KILL spot.

Second Up: The Marry Spot

Get ready, because I'm about to spill an extremely large cup of hot earl grey. Back in my late 20s, I got myself into a situation that I swore I'd never be in: I'd met and fallen in love with a man who was already tied to someone else. I guess I really am one of *those* girls. It began when I started bartending at a popular downtown nightclub and was introduced to my new manager. When we first met, I remember thinking *Karen, you're in trouble.* The attraction was instant, our connection was intense, and I knew without a doubt that we were going to hook up. The guy was perfect for me; he basically checked off all

my boxes (minus the fact that he had a girlfriend and a newborn baby). Our affair lasted for an entire year. Everyone at the club knew about it, since our chemistry was hard to hide. It was a heartbreaking situation for me to be in because I clearly wanted more than he could offer. But the heart wants what the heart wants, right? Not once did I it ever cross my mind that he was a bad guy for cheating (which is strange when I look back on it now). His girlfriend was showing no interest in him and I knew the attention I'd been giving him made him feel wanted and alive. I finally broke things off once I realized that I wanted and deserved something more (which also happened to be the same night my soon-to-be boyfriend, a sexy Maltese guy, walked up to my bar and ordered a Corona with an extra lime). Something good did come out of the experience, though: I learned a valuable lesson about being "the other woman" and vowed never to put myself in that position again. I'm proud to say that after all these years, I have honoured my promise. Attached men are off limits and not on my radar. He's now married to that same woman and shares two children with her. Sadly, he's just as unhappy now as he was back then, and claims to be in a loveless marriage (we've remained friendly over the years and chat occasionally). I don't get it. Why stay? I should have married you," he once said to me. But he's 20 years too late. Although I'm 100% convinced that we would have been great together. To the one that got away . . . for this game, you win the MARRY slot.

Third Up: The Diss Spot

I dated my college professor! Yes, I'm a walking cliché with this one. Whatchathink the odds are that I also experimented with women during this time? Back when I was in college for Radio and Television Broadcasting, I assigned myself an extra-credit assignment and made it my mission to start dating one of my professors. Let's just say that seducing this 30-something, by-the-book, successful afternoon-drive radio host to cross the line and risk his part-time gig at the college kept me entertained between classes. I even chose *Don't Stand So Close to Me* by The Police for an on-air exam once, just to create sexual tension while he graded me. In retrospect, I'm not super proud of my actions, but I was in my early 20s and I still had a lot of growing up to do. We ended up dating for a little over six months. And even though the perks of his AM radio celebrity status, like taking me to see Engelbert Humperdinck with backstage passes, weren't nearly as exciting as the Alanis Morissette concert I got him into for free when she performed at the nightclub where I worked at the time, it was still fun while it lasted. Not surprisingly, the allure of dating him disappeared shortly after graduation, so I chose to forfeit the game altogether. Thankfully, he never did get caught canoodling with a student, and he kept his job. As it turns out, I was just a fetish for him, too; apparently he had a thing for dating students. He ended up breaking policy again and got involved with another student immediately after me (their relationship lasted two years). So based on this questionable move alone, he gets the DISS title. Game over.

Chapter 26

Why I Called the Cops on My Ex-Boyfriend's Daughter

'm not gonna lie . . . calling the police on a 15-year-old girl may have been a bit harsh. But I wanted the virtual smear campaign she had launched against me to stop, and this seemed like the only way. A full year after ending a highly destructive, unstable, and toxic relationship with a man 20 years my senior, it was brought to my attention that his daughter, who was clearly not a fan of mine, was acting on her disdain for me. Being attacked online because of an ex-boyfriend I hadn't once contacted, seen, or even thought about since our final breakup is almost as bananas as the fact that the perpetrator was his young daughter, who'd I never even met!

If his daughter had been able to creep my Instagram, like her mother (the evil ex-wife) used to do, and had seen the new man I had replaced her dad with just a few short months after our breakup, would that have lessened her hate for me? She'd made it pretty clear during my relationship with her father that she thought I was using him as an ATM, so she *spent* the entire year we were together trying to break us up. Rather than trying to develop a real bond with her while I was dating her dad (in retrospect I should have played things differently), I decided to go head-to-head with her after our breakup instead. What choice did I really have? I probably shouldn't have changed my privacy settings and blocked her, interrupting her viewing pleasure and making it impossible for her to see that I'd clearly moved on. Regardless, based on the radio silence between her father and me for almost a year, and the fact that I'd never even once drunk dialed his ass (which is a signature move of mine), it should have been obvious that I was done. Should I have ignored the *#gold digger* and *#bitch* hashtags, the screenshots exposing private texts between her dad and me, or the pics of me she uploaded where she took jabs at my double chin (it was just a bad camera angle, I swear!) that I randomly came across on her TikTok account? Maybe. "She only has a few hundred followers and they're mostly kids So, why do you even care what she thinks?" the officer taking down my statement asked me. "Doesn't someone need to teach her a lesson? And shouldn't I be able to protect my reputation," I challenged him. "What if her next target swallows a bunch of pills, or my name starts trending?" I went on to ask him. Oh wait, my name already was trending. Despite any of the officer's reservations, he agreed to pay the teen culprit a visit.

Daddy, You Have to Wait a Few Days Before Responding

Question: When a father inappropriately involves his young daughter in his personal and very adult relationships and/or his private matters, do you blame the child when she finally snaps and decides to burn the bitch on social media? No. It was hardly the daughter's fault. Her father's to blame, for involving her at all. Based on what I witnessed while we were dating, he'd been grooming her for years to be his loyal confidant and pseudo wife, long before I ever entered the picture. Did I think it was inappropriate when he told me that

he regularly asked his little girl for dating advice, and let her read every text message I sent him, sometimes even letting her write back the responses to me? Hell yes. The drama that ensued after he began painting me to his daughter as an actual

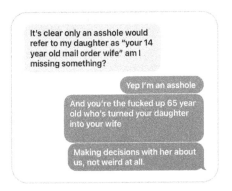

It's clear only an asshole would refer to my daughter as "your 14 year old mail order wife" am I missing something?

Yep I'm an asshole

And you're the fucked up 65 year old who's turned your daughter into your wife

Making decisions with her about us, not weird at all.

threat, though, was far worse than even involving her at all. If you purposely pit your daughter and your girlfriend against each other (narcissists love when people are fighting over them), what do you expect is going to happen? He once gave her $200 not to tell her mother, who also didn't approve of our relationship, that he and I were going on vacation together. "You're paying her to lie for you now? That's so wrong," I said. And he agreed, admitting his motivation behind the bribe was to avoid a fight with his ex-wife. But I overheard him offering her double the next morning when they were on the phone together. Gotta give her props for her negotiating skills. Involving his daughter in our relationship the way he did, and never once defending me when she voiced her false assumptions about me (based on my Instagram page), turned me into an evil step-mama stand-in. If he had acted appropriately, and kept the personal details of his adult relationships private, as they should be (who involves an adolescent in the complexities of an adult romantic relationships?!), what came next could have been avoided.

Total Baller Move

Why was his daughter still posting TikToks about me a year after the split, you ask? *So I fucked your dad for a hot minute. I'm over it. Why aren't you?* And for the record, the "Will File a Police Report" LinkedIn message I sent to him outlining exactly what his daughter was doing and threatening to file a police report if he didn't ensure that it stopped was the only course of action I was planning on taking, assuming she deleted the videos, which in fact she did. If you're wondering why I sent him a LinkedIn message, it was because I was blocked everywhere else! But a week after she deleted the videos, she was back at it again, this time mocking me and my documented love for martinis with a post of her standing in front of STK in Yorkville saying "come get your blue cheese stuffed olives." I'll admit that post was actually pretty hilarious, and I may have laughed out loud. A few days later she uploaded the private LinkedIn message I'd sent her dad warning him to speak to her immediately about her antics towards me or I'd have to take legal action. She captioned it "LMAO, my dad's ex-girlfriend found my TikToks." How she'd even gotten access to this one I have no clue. Was her dad in on it now, too? So, with no real end date in sight to this harassment, and feeling stressed, embarrassed and a little threatened, I called the police and honoured my threat. Ironically, the officer paid them a visit on the eve of Rosh Hashanah, which for Jews signifies a brand new year and a fresh start. Little did they know, as they sat down to celebrate with apples and honey to signify the sweet things to come, that the sour past was about to come knocking on their door.

Was this a case of a disgruntled little girl, or a scorned ex-boyfriend? Not sure. But I highly doubt a 15-year-old girl would be wasting her time and energy on a woman her dad dated years previously, unless perhaps he was encouraging or instigating the bad behaviour. Whatever the reason, I was apparently still very much on her radar, being cyber-bullied by both her and her father (if in fact he was providing her with the ammo), both of whom seemed equally invested and involved. But the adult in this scenario should have known better, and adultifying* his daughter throughout our entire relationship was odd. Perhaps washing her mouth out with soap (or soft-soap if you grew up in my house) the way our parents used to do in the '80s may have helped? "This is one messed-up teen who clearly needs help and a ton of counselling," the officer said to me when he called to follow up. And he was right. I felt awful that I'd involved the authorities, but I'd had no choice. Clearly she was troubled and struggling. And even though her dad was 100% responsible for creating this inappropriate throuple† during our time together by exposing our adult relationship to her when it should have remained private and between us, I had still stayed in the relationship and allowed him to fuck us both in the process (attention JFS‡, this accusation is NOT literal). I couldn't stop him in the end, but I could have walked

. . . .

* Adultify - To treat a child like an adult. Involves children being exposed to adult knowledge and engaging in behaviours understood as adult-like.

† Throuple - A three-way relationship, triad, or closed triad.

‡ JSF—Jewish Family Services.

away sooner so he wouldn't have had material to feed her. She was just a child and just an innocent victim; I blame him entirely. If I ever decide to lift the restraining order and get within 300 feet of her, I might even tell her I'm sorry. But let's be real, I'm probably starring in a secret TikTok account she's created as we speak, after the cop closed the case. Checkmate.

Chapter 27

3 Psychics, 1 Day

. . . .

Deep down I knew I didn't really need a psychic's prediction to tell me that my ex-boyfriend and I had no future together. But I wasn't quite ready to admit that yet, so I prepared myself for my first of three readings, hoping for some . . . hope. With the limited information I'd given the psychic, which included my name, astrological sign, birthdate, and my Bubbie's engagement ring to use as a pendulum, which truth be told I'd been swinging a helluva lot and likely disturbing the shit out of Grams up in heaven, I waited for something good to be revealed. I can't say I got it. But I should have known better than any psychic, tarot deck, or tea leaf that a reconciliation between me and my ex was not in the cards. He'd already made that crystal (ball) clear when we broke up. Yet that didn't stop me from talking to three different psychics in the span of 24 hours, all charging in American dollars, and all delivering their own collection of mostly ambiguous messages from the universe that I wasn't ready to hear. It took me another six months to finally accept their dismal news, which wasn't really news to me at all. But letting go is fucking hard, especially when you're in complete denial that it's even over. And unfortunately, there isn't a magic spell out there that will change this (though one was offered to me for an additional $167.00 USD). Maybe it was the loss of control I felt because it was him who had decided our fate rather than me, that had me feeling so upset. Or maybe it was simply a bruised ego from being rejected. Whatever it was, I desperately needed something to cling to during those harrowing first few months after our breakup. I'm happy to report that I did get past it all, and I later came to realize and accept that he wasn't even worth my time in Canadian currency.

Confessions of a Gentle Stalker

The good news is, I'm finally over my ex, and I now realize that my desperate need for a reconciliation had nothing to do with him. Phew. And to think I'd been reaching out to psychics for answers (deep down I knew they had none) when his deplorable behaviour was all the affirmation I really needed to move on. But like so many other misguided girls out there, I have an incessant need to hold onto things from my past for far longer than I should. And it's pre-destined, I tell ya, dating all the way back to that Monchichi doll I saved for over 30 years so that my future children could enjoy it one day the way I had. My son played with it for less than five minutes before throwing it aside and asking for his iPad back. So much for grand plans, or genetics for that matter. I once had an old flame that I crank-called for an entire year after we broke up (I'm happy to admit that I've somewhat matured since then). Lucky for me, he understood me well and he knew I was an intense, slightly codependent soul, not a dangerous threat in need of a court order. So rather than dismissing all that heavy breathing I gave him at 3 a.m., or not picking up the phone at all, he'd say, "Kare, I know it's you. If you need to talk, just say something and I'll listen." And although I never was brave enough to reveal myself, we both knew I was the culprit, and we still laugh about it to this day. The pattern I'm getting at is that I don't let go easily. I hold on to hope, and I find reasons to stay in the game. So when my friend Claire mentioned a few psychics she'd been contacting lately, and offered up their services (most likely hoping for a referral discount), I was intrigued enough to give one a try. Or more accurately, as DJ Khaled would say, "and another one, and another one."

Not a Good Sign When the Cosmos Tell You to Run

Was it a coincidence that every psychic I spoke to had the exact same thing to say? I guess my ex wasn't the only one who believed we shouldn't be together. But I didn't need a sixth sense or three fairly pricey fortune-teller-y women to tell me this. He'd already provided me with all the free insight I needed. But at the time, soliciting mystical truth-tellers to offer me some advice after we had already broken up seemed like the only option. And all those divinations I received? Well, they ended up being pretty damn accurate. When Psychic Number One said there were things about him that I didn't know, and that he'd been secretly hiding shit, I wasn't surprised in the least. I had only just begun getting to know him after all, and red flags kept creeping up. But when she warned me to stay far away from him, and refused to answer whether or not she "knew" if he still loved me or wanted me back, I deemed her a fake and immediately called Psychic Number Two. But she too instantly said "No Karen, I'm sorry. It's just not in the cards," only a few seconds after drawing mine. "You know he isn't working by choice," she revealed.

"And he won't ever have a job because he doesn't actually want one." Interesting, since I'd not said a word about his employment situation. But that information was pretty irrelevant to me because all I really wanted to know was whether I'd ever hear from him again. At that point it had been months since there'd been any contact. She let me know that in four days, four weeks, four months, or four years I'd hear from him. She said she was certain of it. That's all I needed to hear. Finally, some hope (really, Karen?!). So, with this glimmer of optimism feeding my supernatural high, I decided why not go for a triple fix. When Psychic Number Three mentioned that she saw alcohol and drug abuse, demons that kept him up at night, and lies upon lies surrounding him, all I had to say back was "yeah yeah, but will we ever get back together?" Even the physic had no tolerance for how pathetic I had become. She claimed that my embarrassed guardian angels had just left the room, and then abruptly ended the reading, clearly tired of giving "truth" to those who didn't really want to hear it. She did offer a discount to magically turn him into a nicer person with a potion, though, for if I ever decided to take him back, which she sadly already knew I would. It was rude (and unprofessional?) of her to let me know that it wasn't her psychic ability telling her I'd take him back; "any idiot could see this," she said. Harsh. But she wasn't wrong.

Great Awakenings

FULL DISCLOSURE: I now see that my focus and obsession with getting back together with this particular devil was not about missing him or wanting him back, or even about what was written in the stars. At the time of our breakup, and in the early months that followed, I just couldn't wrap my head around the fact that such a loser—a loser who'd I'd fallen so damn hard for, a loser who had so many problems of his own—was rejecting *me*. His rejection cut away at my self-worth in a way I had not experienced before. It was my self-worth I wanted back, not him. Spoiler alert! I eventually found what I was looking for, without ever seeing him again. I do believe that he was sent to teach me a lesson; one that I needed to learn so I'd never fall for his kind of sorcery again. Men like him can't handle prime real estate, because we remind 'em daily that they're not worthy of a Queen of Cups (my most frequently drawn tarot card) such as us. I didn't need any psychic readings to predict the inevitable outcome, just my own smarts, which I'm proud to say I'm gaining more and more of each day. The only thing that's ever going to fuck him better than I did, is karma. Today almost a year later, I no longer have the urge to contact psychics in bulk anymore, I've removed all the pins from that so called voodoo doll stuffed away in my closet, I've finally found inner peace, formed alliances with other strong women who've dodged the same bullet, and I've accepted the fate of this undestined relationship. And I truly believe our breakup was a blessing in disguise. Now I only pull out the pendulum and call upon my beloved Bubbie for the super important things—like where I last left my car keys!

Chapter 28

Ghosted After Three Years

. . . .

Years ago, when I started hearing about families I knew opening up their homes to international students, I was intrigued
but not sold. Could I allow a stranger to live in my house and sit
on my Crate & Barrel Lounge dream couch? My main concern was
trust, since I had a six-year-old to think about. After my friend Josh
installed secret cameras in his home only to catch one of his visit-
ing students breaking almost every house rule, I wasn't so sure. G-d
help anyone who touches my Kettle One. Right? My friend Sabrina,
who'd hooked up with Kaplan International, had a revolving door
of 20-somethings on short-term stays, and had also experienced a
few issues. I was intrigued, yet hesitant. But after meeting a woman
named Marina on Facebook, who owned a company that brought
exchange students into Canada from the Ukraine, I decided to give it

a try. The students she dealt with were younger, mostly teens attending high school, which was a better fit for my family. Sabrina's students were clubbing, drinking, and smoking in her backyard, which didn't interest me in the slightest. I figured younger high schoolers would be less likely to be in the throes of that stage yet. My main motivation, though, for embarking on the journey of hosting exchange students, aside from the extra cash, was gaining a built-in babysitter. What can I say . . . this single mom's struggle is real! And I desperately wanted to get my martini on. Who knew I'd end up parenting yet another child, on top of the one I was already raising, with my very first occupant.

First up was Dianna, a 15-year-old girl who would be attending Grade 10 in the Fall. She arrived in Canada with her mother that summer, who also moved in with me for a few weeks. While this additional houseguest was definitely not part of the original plan, I relented under the pressure from Marina and allowed it. It worked out fine, though, and both mother and daughter stayed completely out of my way during their joint stay. Once mom left, however, it was a different story altogether. The sweet, innocent, well-behaved teen that had initially rolled in turned into the most miserable and entitled rug rat I'd ever met. Even our sit-down "family" dinners were excruciating, as I'd try to initiate conversation and make her feel at home, with little to no response in return. I'd ask about school, her friends, her interests, her home, but nothing elicited much of a response. When it came to the food I was serving, apparently it wasn't up to her standards, and that Crock-Pot I had dug out of the garage to help prepare dinners for the extra guest wasn't doing the trick. Nothing, and I mean nada (not the Lunchables or even the Bagel Bites) was good enough. When I mentioned she'd have to prepare and pack her own brown-bag lunches for school, she would scowl and go an entire day without eating. When groceries weren't purchased from Whole Foods, I'd catch a faint "blyat" under her breath before she tattled to her mom about the conditions of her living arrangement. If her cereal wasn't organic at $10 a pop, or if anything came out of the freezer (apparently she expected only fresh butcher meat and market fish), a DM in broken English would be waiting in my inbox from her disapproving parents the next day. When she requested Ahi Tuna steaks on a bed of whole-grain wild rice one night for dinner as she rushed out the door one day, I reminded her that this wasn't a hotel, nor a restaurant. "You'll eat what's being served," I said, tossing her a banana so she wouldn't leave empty-handed again. "If you don't like it, make something else, or go to bed hungry." But when Marina told me Diana was telling teachers, family, friends, and her community back home that I'd been starving her, I immediately demanded that she come by and see first-hand my fridge and over-stocked pantry. "Why didn't you send us screenshots of the meals Karen has been providing like I suggested?" Marina asked Diana when we all sat down to discuss. "Are you kidding me? You actually believe her?" I said. After some investigation and a heated Ukrainian discussion between Diana and Marina that I wasn't privy to, Diana admitted to making the whole thing up so she could justify moving out of my place and rooming with a classmate instead (whose parents had already agreed to take her in for some extra income of their own). I sent her packing that night. And although I was pissed for weeks about the whole ordeal, and worried about my reputation, months later Marina informed me that Diana got caught cheating on a final exam and was sent packing on the next flight back home. Chez Zman was once again open for business. Hopefully to a better houseguest next time. Cha-ching.

Boys Versus Girls

"How about taking in a 16-year-old boy this time?" Marina asked a couple months after Diana left. "He's super respectful and comes from a good family." I had no problem with a male student, so I quickly agreed to it. My only trepidation was being eaten out of house and home, which I'm told teenage boys are known to do. But it turns out I had nothing to worry about, since Dani didn't eat much at all, or at least not at my place. I later found out that he'd been secretly ordering Uber Eats daily, charging everything to his parents' account without their permission. After mentioning that his personal chef back home was world-renowned, I was reminded that these kids were filthy rich and probably used to "better" things than I was able to offer. So, I decided to up my "dark-Walmart-meat-because-it's-cheaper" game and renew my Costco membership. It's the least I could do. Frankly, it was probably the *only* thing I could do to bring things up a notch. Kudos to me for trying, right? White meat or not, there were hardly any complaints or issues the entire time Dani was with me. Based on my experience, boys are the way to go, and they're my personal preference if I ever decide to do this again. Yes, Dani was loud AF, and he was constantly playing online games while screaming at his computer screen in a foreign language. But I totally get it; Tour of Duty is intense. Plus, I'm the mother of a now 10-year-old boy, so listening to anyone other than *Flamingo* on You-Tube (my son's all-day, every day go-to source of entertainment during COVID) is a step up! Trust me.

During Dani's stay, I also welcomed a 19-year-old named Anna into our home, who ended up staying for three years. Her situation was completely different than the previous students. She was already a Canadian resident, attending college, fluent in English, and had a part-time job. Basically, she was self-sufficient. And my son and I loved the shit out of her, almost 'til the very end. She ate meals with us, attended scary movie nights, celebrated birthdays and holidays, and even shared my Spotify and Amazon Prime accounts. For all intents and purposes, she was family. And although she was technically an adult, I was still old enough to be her mother, and I expected the same level of respect from her that my son showed me (most of the time!). Sometimes, though, the lines would get blurred between "friend" and "landlord" and she'd forget who she was talking to. Once after returning home from a night out with the old man, she scolded me and told me to go to my room because apparently I was too drunk and annoying to deal with as I fumbled to pay her. The next morning I made it very clear that she was never to speak to me like that again. Months later, after adamantly saying NO to her request for a pet bird, she brought Luna home anyway and expected me to take care of it, sometimes for up to two months at a time when she went back home for a visit. I didn't want to ruffle any feathers and lose my dirt-cheap babysitter, or the extra monthly rent income for that matter, so I never said a word, fed the damn bird, and cleaned its shit up—and I hate to admit it, but I became her bitch.

I have a few regrets about some of my decisions during my time as host to these exchange students, but my biggest regret was saying yes when Anna asked if her friend Valeria could move into Dani's old room following his departure. Because once they got a taste of what life could be like as roommates without any rules, they stopped following any of mine and decided to leave. They were 22 years old at this point, so I'd known this day was coming—I just didn't expect it to happen just a few short months after the plus-one walked in. When they said they'd found a two-bedroom apartment in a very expensive part of the city for $1,100/mo, where rent is usually at least double that, I was skeptical. When I asked for the address a few days later, Anna claimed she couldn't remember. "You don't know where you're moving to?" I laughed. "I'm asking because your fees sound too good to be true, so I'm just curious". She knew she'd been caught in a lie, so she backpedalled and revealed that their new rent was actually $2,300/mo. My place was $1,000 including food, WiFi and everything else factored in, so things just didn't add up. I guess it was no longer fun at Chez Zman anymore.

After my friend Leslie welcomed an exchange student named Lola into her home for a couple of years, Lola became her adopted daughter. Leslie's entire family even traveled to the Ukraine one summer for three weeks, on Lola's parents' dime, when they graciously treated them all to plane tickets. But after deciding she'd rather live on campus at the university she was attending, and adopt an expensive toy poodle, Lola left without proper notice, and Leslie hasn't heard a single word from her since. The lesson here? These kids are tenants, not family, even though it's gonna feel like so much more. So don't be fooled. I made the mistake of making Anna a part of my family and treating her like a daughter, but she didn't even say goodbye the day she moved out. And just like Leslie and her student, I haven't heard from Anna since. Adding insult to injury, Anna unfollowed me on Instagram too. My middle-age antics get a lot of likes and positive comments, I swear!

Tenants First. Not Family

Recently I tried reaching out to Anna, asking if she could reply back to my son who'd attempted contacting her via text a number of times with no response. I tried explaining to her that he was just a child and couldn't comprehend what he'd done wrong to justify being ignored, so if she could perhaps shoot him a quick "hello" it would mean a lot to him. My request didn't seem like a big ask, especially after all I'd done for her and the relationship we'd shared for years. Unfortunately, Anna is a child and chose not to respond (to either of us), teaching my son that not all relationships stick. This is a lesson I don't think he needed to learn quite yet. To this day I still don't understand why she ghosted me after three years of being in each other's lives and sharing a warm relationship throughout. Bottom line: if you can treat these foreign exchange students as income only, or simply as a way to get that BMW X3 you've been eyeing, without ever getting too close or blurring the lines between "friend" and "renter," you're good to go. Would I open my house to foreign exchange students again? Hell yeah. But next time I welcome anyone inside, I open my front door only, and not my heart.

Chapter 29

The Plus-One Dilemma

When my friend Daphne invited me to her wedding without a date (shout-out to her and her hubby Justin who are still together and living happily in LA with their two children—#rare), I didn't go all bat-shit crazy. Yes, people, I was very much single at the time, but I also knew everyone at my table, so no biggie. Right? Even Rebecca, the girl who dissed me on my answering machine when we were kids if you recall, had gotten married and was there with her husband, so it was all good. And looking back, I was surrounded by familiar faces and friends so it should not have been the issue it ultimately turned out to be. But during the newlyweds' first dance, when the DJ got on the mic and invited everyone to come join the happy couple, my entire table—which consisted only of couples—got up to get their Hall & Oates on. As the only single person there, I was left completely alone. And it was at this precise moment that I realized the importance of having a plus one. At first, I tried to look busy, spreading a semi-frozen butter square onto a soft piece of challah without any success. iPhones weren't a thing yet, so I couldn't post a selfie fake pretending to be happy. I sat there feeling like a complete loser for as long as I could stand it, but eventually I just ran to the bathroom and locked myself in a stall. And as I sat there on the toilet, feeling extra sorry for myself, without any party favours to numb the pain (this would come later in my 30s), I began to cry. Because I too wanted someone by my side; some arm candy of my own, to have and to hold, and take advantage of the open bar with—it was a Jewish wedding after all! Although the newlyweds had no idea that one of their guests was even missing for most of the night, or that attending their wedding solo would end up having such a significant future impact on me, this marked the first and also the very last time I would ever attend a party alone.

Who invites a grown-ass adult woman to a formal sit-down dinner event by herself anyway? As it turns out, statistically speaking, lots of people do. And for those of you who don't know . . . it's tacky as fuck. So, for all you women out there who haven't met your future husband(s) yet, or are in between situationships (realistically more my case), and are invited to an event without a plus one, sending back your RSVP with a big fat NO is perfectly acceptable. Plus, it sends a clear message to anyone still pulling this sort of crap that it's not okay. And no, you won't experience FOMO.* I promise you'll be just fine. While it's an easy rule to make for yourself, it can get awkward when it's a really good friend doing the inviting you solo thing. Many moons ago my BFF JoJo graciously invited me to her daughter's Bat Mitzvah, without a date. I didn't know how to handle

. . . .

* FOMO—Fear of Missing Out.

the situation. Should I say something to her or should I stay quiet? Maybe offer to pay for the extra plate? I knew I couldn't just let it go, so I took a deep breath, prepared myself for an extremely uncomfortable conversation, and picked up the phone. Why should I be punished just because no one currently liked it enough to put a ring on it? Still, in retrospect I should have just sucked it up and gone solo, or not attended at all. And putting JoJo in that very awkward position of feeling bad for having not thought to include a plus-one for me, which she was quick to amend I might add (what choice did she have at that point?), should never have happened. To this day I still feel horrible about it, but I learned a valuable lesson. Now I just bow out gracefully when I'm invited to something alone. A few years back, my good friend Emma sent me an invitation to her wedding which was being held an hour's drive outside of Toronto. When she said I couldn't bring a date because she was cutting costs and keeping her special day to only 60 guests, I messaged her to explain why I couldn't attend. And I was in a serious relationship at the time, which made it even more inappropriate and downright wrong. But she desperately wanted me there, so despite the fact that she was trying to keep the guest list small, she said I could bring him anyway, making me pinky swear not to tell any of the single gals at the table. Do I feel guilty now for bringing the old man along and then dumping him a few months later? Sure. But having someone there beside me, a plus one of my very own, to eat the burnt tilapia that I'd paid for off my plate (I'd made sure to cover the cost of both of us, on top of the overly generous wedding gift), and to whisper sweet "you may want to cool it on the vodka soda" nothings in my ear, really did mean the world to me. So thank you, Em, for making that exception.

Confusing Plus-One with Being The One

While having a plus-one can often be the difference between a great time or a mediocre one, it's important to also remember that bringing along an insignificant person just to stand beside you isn't always what it's cracked up to be. So, don't be fooled by the false sense of security of having a hand to hold when you walk in. Depending on WHO your plus one is, it can sometimes be just as lonely, if not more so, than attending an event alone. When my sexy Maltese boyfriend John, who at the time I thought was the one, included me in every dinner party he hosted while we were together, it didn't mean shit. I'm pretty sure none of his guests even knew we were a couple. But why would they? John would make a point of sitting nowhere near me at dinner, and then would ignore me for the remainder of the night, playing host to everyone else at the party. He did this every single time, at every party we ever attended together. When I stormed out one night after I'd finally had enough, he didn't even notice I was missing until the next morning. And it's shit like this that I've carried with me and allowed to affect my subsequent relationships. When I recently attended a Bat Mitzvah with my last serious boyfriend, my old baggage reared its ugly head. When we got to our assigned table, he tried pawning me off on his buddy's wife so he could sit beside his friend instead, which instantly brought me back to all those hurtful evenings at John's. And at that moment I realized that even with a plus-one by your side, you can still feel like you're solo. It matters WHO your plus-one is, too, so choose wisely, girls. If you're not going to enjoy any of the benefits of bringing a plus-one, there's no point having to suffer through the awkward conversation with the host that invited you without one (if you dare say something), or shell out extra money to cover the cost of a plate your guest will be too busy with others to even eat. Sometimes it's better to attend a party solo (if you're feeling bold), or not attend at all, than show up with a plus-one who makes you feel like you're solo anyway.

Exceptions to Our Rules

When my cousin Sammy, who I'm extremely close with, called me up recently to ask if I'd reconsider my plus-one rule for her upcoming wedding, of course I said yes. It was COVID, after all, so it's only fair. There are obviously exceptions to the rule, and a worldwide pandemic calls for one. When her wedding was originally planned, before COVID and lockdowns and rules about large gatherings, I'd been invited with my ex (who I was dating at the time), and I really appreciated that she was including a guy I'd only been with for a few months. But when the pandemic hit and her June 2020 wedding was postponed, it all became a moot point. Due to number restrictions, their new plan was a very small outdoor gathering with fewer than 100 people. I understood the need to whittle down the invite list; she was having to cut friends and family, so I certainly didn't think my plus-one should make the cut. So, I agreed to step out of my comfort zone and attend solo. He'd broken up with me by then, so it's not like he would have accompanied me. This would make it the first time in 20 years that I'd be attending a party on my own. Breathe, Karen; long, deep breaths. To be honest, I was looking forward to seeing how everything might unfold. Isn't it a known fact that weddings are a great place to pick up single men too? Unfortunately, their nuptials were axed yet again (thanks to the second lockdown) and rescheduled for the summer of 2022. Hopefully by then this whole deadly virus thing will be over, and/or enough of us will be vaccinated so that number restrictions will be a thing of the past or, more importantly, I'll have a new man in my life. Ha. Well, here's hoping, right?

So, let's all raise a glass and make a celebratory toast to my future boyfriend, sidekick and next plus-one; the man who will essentially be responsible for giving me an out so I don't have to follow through and attend her shindig by myself as promised. Oh, and to the amazing time we're obviously going to have together as one. Cheers!

Please Return to Sender

To all the women out there still accepting invites to parties without a plus-one, just stop. We single gals deserve the same benefits that our married or coupled-up friends receive. And every guest should be treated the same. If we're not, I say blame the host. And for every host out there still doing this? Please end the torture now. Yes, I will make an exception every once in a while, if it means making someone else's big day. It shouldn't always be about me, right? Or should it? But if you mail me a fancy invitation, or deliver one right to my door (with butterflies included in the box), or send me an e-invite without a plus-one attached, I'm likely a NO-SHOW, regardless of how great the chicken fingers will taste at the kids table you've already assigned me to. And although part of growing up means sometimes doing things we don't want to do, as adults we always have a choice. Hasn't my social anxiety been through enough? So, if you've recently gotten engaged (congrats to my sister!) or are planning your next big bash without including a plus-one in my invite, that *Wedding Crasher* you see over there double fisting by the bar . . . he's with me!

Chapter 30

Betting on Black,
and Winning

. . . .

When I got recruited by BlackBerry, formally known as Research In Motion (RIM), I didn't know it would ultimately end up being such a windfall. I'm certain they didn't either. But giving me the boot immediately after I announced that I was pregnant, and then gambling on whether or not I'd take action, was their one fatal mistake and my unexpected gain. You can't axe a person after revealing something like this! Think of the PR scandal, all the bad press, not to mention the social media coverage—Twitter would blow up! Clearly, they had no idea who they were messing with. Hello, have you met me? All it took was a 30-second phone call with a lawyer claiming he had already won my case to get me started. Ultimately, their mistake gave me the opportunity to enjoy an entire year of maternity leave with my newborn son, without having to worry about cash or my next move. So, thank you, RIM. The experience ended up giving me the gift of time, which is a luxury most new moms, especially single ones, often can't afford. But seriously, RIM, a bit harsh don't you think? Breaking up with me after I'd already purchased the townhouse near the office so we could be closer together? Let's not forget that YOU chased ME, even after I refused to drive 60 minutes for the initial interview. But you pleaded and pushed and wouldn't give up. And I get it; big city talent is hard to find, with not many folks willing to pack up and leave for the much smaller city where you're located. But you were relentless, and eventually won ($$$) me over. And not to toot my own horn, but all those witty headlines I created for you (e.g., *GRAB A PIECE OF THE π*) were pretty damn impressive don't ya think?, so what the actual F was the problem? It really didn't have to end this way, although I'm now glad it did.

Working For a Misogynist

When my boss Darren, who was super easy-going with the sexiest British accent I'd ever heard, asked me to pop by his desk so I could meet Yves from the brand department, I didn't think much of it. Yves was new, and introductions were commonplace. But when I stepped into his office, bad energy occupied the entire room. The fact that Yves was also a carbon copy of actor Christoph Waltz, who played a Nazi in *Inglourious Basterds*, didn't help. The resemblance was uncanny. And although I couldn't put my finger on exactly why I was getting such negative vibes (it wasn't just his resemblance to Hollywood evil), I knew something was off. When Darren mentioned later that he was thinking of bringing Yves on as Creative Director, I blurted out, "Big mistake! There's something about him that I just don't trust, he's disingenuous." "The offer's already been set *in motion*, no pun intended Karen," he joked. "I promise, it's a good decision for all of us." A few weeks later we received the official announcement that Yves would be joining the team. Little did I know that day that the arrival of Yves would ultimately lead to the downfall of my cushiony, close-to-six-figure job, with perks such as three WFH days a week and that free clunker of a BlackBerry phone (which was actually a pretty hot commodity in its time if you can believe anything other than Apple ever monopolized the tech industry). Turns out that I wasn't the only one who was in trouble. None of the women on the team were safe, and we would soon find out that Yves was a misogynist, clearly evident in his treatment of the women on our team, in comparison to the men, and how we were all dropping like flies while every Tom, Dick and Harry remained gainfully employed. It appeared that this small-town born and raised Creative Director, who dreamed of one day moving to the city and making it big in Toronto, was threatened by women; and especially me because I was both a woman and a talented big-city import.

Yves' first underhanded attempt to push me out came when he pulled me aside one afternoon to say that he now needed me in the office five days per week. Really? "You are a valued member of the company, Karen, and it's a waste that you aren't here more often," he lied. "But my three WFH days are written in my contract, Yves," I said, making sure to over-emphasize the silent S in his name that he often corrected me on, and I knew he hated. "Well, things change," he said, hoping this would force me to quit. But I didn't. Game on, Yves. The first thing I did was go to HR and tell them I observed Shabbat (the Jewish Sabbath), asking if I could keep my Friday WFH day for "religious reasons" (clever, right?) which they had no choice but to let me do. Yves was furious.

A few weeks later, my work suddenly needed his approval before being sent off to stakeholders, when I had always had clearance to send my work directly to the client before. He then began rewriting my ads, adding in bold text and all-caps, "THIS IS THE WORST COPY I'VE EVER READ, HERE ARE MY CHANGES" to every email subject header. Months later when I sent him back his own re-written work for sign-off, and he sent me back, "THIS IS THE WORST ONE YET," I was thrilled to respond with "Um really? YOU ACTUALLY WROTE THIS ONE YVESSS," making sure to cc Darren on the thread. Understandably, this didn't go over too well. After this little incident, he ramped up the daily harassment. If I left a meeting to use the washroom, he'd run to Darren claiming that I was on a personal call. If I didn't agree with what he said, he'd cite me for insubordination. If I came into the office a few minutes late because of a pile-up on the highway, he'd issue me a written warning. Then he started messing with my yearly performance review, making shit up, and putting me on probation. He was clearly out to get me, and the stress was starting to take a toll on my mental health. At the time, I was trying for a baby and worried that it might not happen now because of him.

After several months and countless official complaints made to HR about his unprofessional behaviour, his subpar managerial capabilities, his mistreatment of (mostly) women and the hostile work environment he'd created, Yves was finally demoted, and we all went back to reporting directly to Darren. Meaning, Yves could no longer boss us around, torment us or harass us. While this was great news for me, things were about to get personal.

Protecting My Piece of the π

Although Yves had been officially taken down by a group of strong women who worked under him (almost 90% of the complaints launched against him came from women, with a few male colleagues who tried to help), and he was now walking around the office with his (tiny) dick between his legs and no actual authority, he still found ways to make our lives miserable, and I knew my days were inevitably numbered. *It's only a matter of time before he steals one of my winning ideas or makes me take the fall for something I didn't do,* I thought (both of which did in fact eventually happen just as predicted). So, I did what any smart and strategic employee would do; I went to Human Resources to let 'em know that I was pregnant. At least now I knew I was safe. Discrimination against women in the workplace was on the rise at the time, and companies were taking extra precautions to avoid accusations of that nature. Think #metoo, but 10 years ago in its infancy. If they fired me now for any reason, I could say that the timing seemed suspect, and I'd almost definitely have a case. It wasn't a secret that Yves was upset about inheriting a team of people that he didn't get to handpick himself. At this point, Darren had resigned and wasn't around to protect any of us anymore. Plus, having just watched my co-worker and good friend Aleah get fired for no reason, I knew I needed the extra leverage. A few days later I got called into a boardroom and, you guessed it, got served my walking papers. Effective immediately. "Sorry, Karen, we are making some changes. Please return your BlackBerry and be on your way," the CEO, who was clearly on "Team Yves," said. At this point I had nothing more to lose, so I gave them a little taste of what it looks like to fuck with a woman growing a tiny human being inside of her belly. "You're asking me to hand in my phone when you know that I'm 'with child' and have a 45-minute highway drive ahead of me? What if something happens to me or the baby and I can't contact anyone for help?" I slyly asked. He then stormed out of the room with our HR rep, only to immediately return and say I could keep the damn device. His way of saying "make all the long-distance phone

LET'S TALK ABOUT EX, BABY

calls you want on your drive home," right? Setting *in motion . . .* my sweet revenge.

Do large corporations with deep pockets like BlackBerry (pre-2016, of course) actually get away with this crap? The answer is yes. And by crap, I mean discriminating against women in the workplace, and/or proceeding with wrongful terminations, or in cases like mine, firing an employee after she announces she's pregnant hoping that we'll do nothing. During my termination meeting they claimed it had zero to do with my pregnancy and that I was in fact the problem, not Yves, even though he had countless complaints already filed against him. Whatever their reasons were for getting rid of me that day, doing it immediately following my big reveal didn't help their case. It ended up helping my case. I guess Black-Berry didn't really know me all that well (even after all that wooing and three years of loyal service). I don't intimidate easily, even if the company I'm going up against is mega huge, which is what they were hoping for and banking on. A week later when my lawyer called RIM about the pending lawsuit I had filed against them, they agreed to settle right then and there. And although I'm not really allowed to discuss the exact details of my case, let's just say that they were forced to put me back on the payroll for the duration of my pregnancy (six months), and they further doled out an extremely large lump sum settlement. I'm guessing they didn't want to deal with the bad press, or harm their reputation, even though it was pretty clear to everyone that this had nothing to do with a baby. So, was that year of unwarranted office harassment at the hands of Yves worth it? Yes. It started a chain of events that would ultimately lead me to where I wanted and needed to be. Which was at home with my child and not tied to a company that was about to fold anyway. Ironically, about a year or so later, 75% of RIM employees permanently lost their jobs,

Yves included, and the company tanked. And to this day, Yves still lives life in the small town he always hoped to leave, working at a small cybersecurity company, likely still dreaming of moving to the big city and one day coming out on top. And I like to imagine people are still mispronouncing his name, emphasizing the silent S with vigour and intent.

Chapter 31

My Infinite Playlist

. . . .

I f music heals the soul, I think I've been on an extremely spiri-
tual journey as of late, possibly even guru-worthy. It's certainly
a far healthier option than my usual dirty martini escape, which
often ends in a regrettable drunk dial. Be strong, Karen, be strong.
So instead of scrolling through my liquor cabinet, I've been scrolling through my various playlists, choosing to mix it up with music
rather than booze. Music's been a great friend to me lately, helping
me get lost and forget about the things I cannot change, and remind
myself that everything happens for a reason, even if we can't always
see the bigger picture just yet. So every evening, and always post
break-up, I get into my car, connect my favourite Spotify playlist, and
just drive. Sometimes for hours at a time. My solo car jam sessions
are damn safer than running back to a man who's done hitting play
or pressing repeat.

My Usual Routine

1. Listen to sad songs (Adele makes the list, naturally)
2. Feel extremely sorry for myself
3. Ugly cry (even though I still look pretty)
4. Do a drive-by (I mean, a McDonalds drive-thru)
5. Play empowering songs
6. Send an "empty bubble" text by *mistake* to grab attention
7. Listen to sexually/explicit songs that make me feel like the Sexiest Pringle Alive (thanks, Riri)
8. Send a booty-call text to my current go-tos
9. Proceed with previous step depending on who's answered the late night bling
10. Head home and take a hot bubble bath . . . or a cold shower (as of late)

This routine can be a dangerous cycle for someone like me, who's extremely lyrically driven; if the lyrics get too intense, I get distracted and end up in a spiral of sadness and self-pity. I also have this horrible habit of skipping through songs on purpose, trying to find the most depressing one, and then ugly-crying in private. I know I'm not the only person who does this. I also know I'm not the only person guilty of re-reading every text message I've ever sent to whatever ex I'm currently thinking about (yes, even while driving), unless I've accidentally erased them all, which I've done. If there are no text messages to review, then it's back to just replaying only the good memories I've still got lingering around in my head, and then repressing everything else. Here's a peek into my awesome (somewhat dated, but still relevant) playlists:

Boyfriend, Ariana Grande & Social House

"But you don't want me to see anybody else"

Here's a song that brings me back to my 20s, when dating commitment-phobes, bartending at Whiskey Saigon, chasing aloof men and getting high off the hot and cold drama was in style. But that was then, and this is now. And although "I'm still a motherfucking train wreck," I will no longer give my time to anyone who doesn't really want it. Am I still kicking myself 20 years later for trying so hard, overcompensating, appearing utterly desperate and hooking up with losers who were never worth my time? Guilty. So if you're a grown-ass player (you know who you are) still pulling this kind of shit, please grab your Nirvana tee and CAMELS off the floor and shut the door on your way out. I'm now masquerading as a strong, grown-ass independent woman, who knows exactly what she wants and won't settle for anything less anymore. Let's see how this goes.

Someone Like You, Van Morrison

"I've been doing some soul searching to find out where you're at"

This has been a favourite since the early '90s when it was featured in Bridget Jones's Diary. The hopeless romantic in me is still waiting for *my* Mark Darcy to appear (no, it wasn't you). Because nothing says real-life like your guy bolting out of his backlogged-in-traffic Uber so he can run to the airport on foot in the pouring rain just to stop you from getting on a plane, or blasting *In Your Eyes* from a boombox outside your window, or saving you from a rolling garbage bin when your Gucci shoe gets caught in a sewer cover (à la Jennifer Lopez in *The Wedding Planner*), right? Well, a girl can dream. Instead, I'm the girl who accepted a medium dark roast from Tim

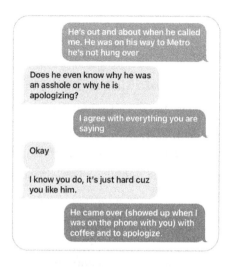

He's out and about when he called me. He was on his way to Metro he's not hung over

Does he even know why he was an asshole or why he is apologizing?

I agree with everything you are saying

Okay

I know you do, it's just hard cuz you like him.

He came over (showed up when I was on the phone with you) with coffee and to apologize.

Hortons as a peace offering after my boyfriend and I got into our first fight. And rather than listening to my gut (or every friend who said he didn't deserve a second chance) and breaking up with him the very next morning, I sipped on the warm beverage he showed up with unannounced, mistaking this as the "grand gesture" I'd been waiting for (I blame every rom-com), and took him upstairs to the bedroom instead. Um . . . maybe holding out for a guy more like the fictional characters we all see on screen is the better way to go.

Sex with Me, Rihanna

"Stay up off my Instagram, pure temptation"

Okay folks, now THIS is my anthem. Need I say more? And I own it; every G-ddamn inch. Even when I'm way too tired and only have the energy to starfish! Jokes aside, this song oozes sex appeal and gets me in the mood every time (which truth be told doesn't take much). And I've introduced it to everyone! So "wrap up your drugs and come make me happy." Because *Sex with Me* really is . . . AMAZING. But what if *he's* not amazing (in that department)? What then? Do we suck it up, or do we move on? This is a burning (not to be confused with itchy) question that's come up a few times with men from my past. For me, the sex doesn't need to be mind-blowing. Blow my mind instead. That's right, you heard me correctly—send me a nice text, treat me RIGHT, make me feel loved, desired and 100% secure in our relationship. That's the real turn-on. Once I had a boyfriend who couldn't "get it up" because he was high as a "muthafucka" after he'd taken a bunch of drugs. So, we stayed up the entire night talking and kissing instead. Honestly, it was 10 times more intense and powerful than any sex-marathon we'd ever had. So you see, sex doesn't actually have to be amazing

every time. But finding a guy who's willing to go the extra mile and at least try to make things great (even on the off nights) will always leave a lasting impression and keep us coming back for more.

Pumpkin, Tricky ft. Alison Goldfrapp

"You go your way and I'll see mine. Feels like wasted time"

Once you hear this song and experience this kind of intensity, there's no turning back. It was 1998 and I was bartending at RPM nightclub when I saw this concert. With muted sensuality and erotica dripping from the stage, my goosebumps never stood a chance. It's still one of the most powerful duets I've ever seen performed live, and they didn't make eye contact once. I desperately want and need this in my life. But this song isn't actually about healthy love. Not one bit. I had no clue. And that connection I witnessed on stage? The one so sharp it could literally cut through glass? Well, it was toxic. According to psychologists, toxic attachments created by repeated physical or emotional trauma with intermittent positive reinforcement are temporary and not real. So don't be fooled by this false sense of attachment. Healthy intense love affairs are nurtured with intimacy, warmth and positivity. They are the only connections worth pursuing. Have a listen, note the difference, and see what I mean.

Bad, Wale ft. Rihanna

"'Cause I had some issues, I won't commit"

This song is sort of twofold for me. On the one hand, I feel like the strongest, sexiest, baddest biatch alive when I'm blasting it. But it also reminds me that I too have some issues of my own to deal with; issues that have prevented me from letting my guard down. As a result, I've chosen men that don't bring anything to the table. And even though I'm in my 40s now and should know better when it comes to romance, there's still that little girl inside of me that wants to be swept off her feet. Thankfully, we grow up, move on, and hopefully learn from past mistakes; it's not like we have a choice. But I still want to go back and give myself a great big hug, and maybe a little shake for all those past mistakes.

Beautiful, Snoop Dogg ft. Pharrell

"I asked you nicely, don't make the dog lose it"

Is there anything better than knowing you're someone's favourite girl? That you possess the kind of power that makes him lose his mind whenever you're around? The answer is no. There's nothing better than feeling forever adored. This is how it should always be in a relationship, not just at the beginning. So when their feelings change, we gals always know. When I first met my ex, my phone calls were

always answered on the first ring. He would even regularly diss his own mother whenever my name popped up on his call-display. Towards the end, however, our conversations felt more like forced obligation, or he'd send me straight to voice-mail rather than chat with the giddy adolescent excitement I was used to receiving. Once when I called him up at mid-night so I could be the first to wish him a happy birthday, he seemed extremely distant and cold. *Clearly, he doesn't want to talk,* I assumed. When I brought it up, he immediately gaslit me and made me feel crazy for even thinking such a ridiculous thought. But my intuition turned out to be right. He was secretly on his way to a bud's place during the first lockdown when we were all urged to stay at home and annoyed that he'd been caught. So much for breaking the rules for me! In fact, COVID was often the excuse he'd use NOT to spend time with me, even though we had just gotten back together. And once this became a broken record, he started using my own son, who was having some attach-ment issues at the time, as his excuse, limiting our hangouts to set two-hour time slots whenever I went to his place, "for my son's sake." Of course, I tried convincing myself that I was just overanalyzing and needed to chill the fuck out. But during this time, he also stopped initiating plans altogether, meaning that whenever we did get to-gether, it was always me who suggested it. If a guy isn't putting in the time or effort anymore, and you're always left questioning how he really feels, nine times out of 10 he's already checked out. The best relationships are the ones where you feel adored months and years in, the very same way you did at the beginning. The ones where you can completely be yourself and he still thinks you're amazing both inside and out, no matter what. So, if he's not looking at you the way you're always looking at him, it's time to choose a different song.

Bad Intentions, Niykee Heaton ft. Migos

"I got some secrets I forgot to mention, haven't learned my lesson"

I've added this song for all my male readers. And although the power of the pussy is a definite undertone in this video, this song is actually about empowerment. It's knowing what you want and going out and getting it. Because being a sexy bad-ass bitch and having men fight over you is great, but being a confident Pringle and standing on your own two feet is 10 times better.

At Last, Etta James

"And here we are in heaven, for you are mine at last"

I've been obsessed with blues, R&B, soul and Motown music ever since I can remember, so when a guy I'd never met but was headed out on a first date with bought tickets for us to see Etta James, I secretly thought I'd hit the jackpot. During the concert, I turned to him, looked deep into his eyes and said "I'm so happy right now," clearly expressing my excitement for being in the presence of such a great music legend. His response? "You're amazing too, and I look forward to our future." Oops. Definitely not what I meant. Months later I ran into him at a vegan restaurant (during one of my no-meat phases) with his new girlfriend who was wearing, no joke, a fox fur! Fast forward 20 years to the present day, when my EX invited me to meet up with him and some friends for drinks at Hemmingway's post-breakup. If you can believe it, that same guy I went to the Etta James concert with so many years ago was right there sitting at our table! Now unhappily married to the same fur coat lady, he went on to disrespect his marriage, my breakup which was still fresh, and his good friend (my ex), by sticking his tongue down my throat after my ex left to continue his night elsewhere. The next morning when I texted my ex to tell him about what had happened, instead of getting upset at his disloyal bud, or caring that my lips had touched someone else's, his response was priceless. And it was his reply that really spoke volumes. Because after months of pretending that he was still interested in trying again, his dismissive text back to me, saying that "everybody wants a good kiss," ultimately, finally, and likely inadvertently on his part, revealed his true feelings. And it certainly wasn't interest.

> Oh and Your married friend Kissed me yesterday when we were leaving- I told you there's absolutely no bro code when it comes to women
>
> Everyone wants a good kiss

What he said was the nail in the coffin, the final straw that sealed the deal and ended the torment. Every reach-out he's sent thereafter, wishing me a happy Halloween (is that even a thing?!) or happy birthday, has been left unread, and we haven't spoken since.

H.A.T.E U. (Having A Typical Emotional Upset)
Mariah Carey

"And I wish I can press reset and feel that feeling again"

Of course it isn't a Sexypringle playlist without my Mimi; everyone knows that. And this song, written for every woman out there waiting for the pain from a breakup to quickly turn to hate so we can just get on with our lives, is one of those ballads I keep on high rotation. A year ago, when I originally wrote this chapter, I would have said

"nope, that's never going to happen," since I'm the girl who unequivocally can't let go. But today while editing, I can now say with 100% confidence that I've moved on with my life. And the ex I didn't think I'd ever be able to get over? Well, I'm happy to say that I'm over him, although at times I still get triggered if someone mentions his name. I'm only human after all. Hate though? That's a strong word, and I've got too much respect for my late Bubbie, who taught me never to use it, to start singing those praises now. Plus hating him gives him power, which he definitely doesn't deserve (no one should invoke ANY feelings that strong). I'll admit that I did at one point, early on post-breakup, have *A Typical Emotional Upset (H.A.T.E.U.)* where he was concerned, just like Mariah Carey has in this song. Did I feel schadenfreude? Not exactly. But knowing that it also hadn't worked out with the girl he hooked up with immediately after me did lessen my pain a teeny tiny bit. I'm not gonna lie. It's funny how that works. Wounds do heal, however; even the ones that cut deep. So as Ariana would say (is Mariah still feuding with her?) "Thank U, Next."

Baby, I'm Yours, Breakbot ft. Irfane

"Won't you understand, your wish is my command"

I'm ending this with an homage to all the songs we simply can't listen to anymore because they're associated with a memory, good or bad. I used to love this song because my boyfriend at the time and I would listen to it on repeat. We discovered Breakbot together, and it was our "go-to" whenever we got home from a night out. And although it's been almost two years since we broke up, whenever I hear one of his songs, I need to turn it off. It's just not the same anymore. When I hear it now, I'm reminded that obsessive love isn't actually real love, it's codependency. I'm working hard, though, to rewire my thoughts and recognize what a healthy relationship looks like. When I'm having trouble and I start reverting to my old ways, I just hit SKIP and try to forget we ever happened. So many amazing jams in my playlist are now ruined! Whether it's a memory that triggers pain, happiness or even love—if it's associated with another person, and that person is no longer in my life—it really does kind of suck. But music can teach us so many valuable lessons if we pull over onto a side street and really take a listen. And that's why it will forever remain a constant in my life. And hey, if Chelsea Handler can break old patterns, ditch the bad boys and finally find true love with comedian Jo Koy, then so can I!

Chapter 32

Corona-Palooza

. . . .

Although I'm hopeful that this *Apocalypse Now* vibe will soon be over, I'm not holding my breath. Our new way of life is turning the absurd into the acceptable. My second COVID birthday is fast approaching, and I still haven't decided what I'm ordering from Uber Eats, or who's going to be on my Zoom call if I choose to even bother with that this time around. During the second lockdown, I considered driving 45 minutes out of my way to a restaurant outside my area code (without the same restrictions) just so I could sit inside a shitty steak-and-seafood house and eat. Am I nuts? After learning that these establishments were asking for proof of address, though (to catch any out-of-towners), I decided against it. With so many emerging trends taking place because of COVID, it seems only fitting to take a look at what some of them are. Plus, these trends have been such a big part of my life while writing this memoir (Amazon Top Pick?!), it seems silly not to discuss them. So, while we wait for my book to inevitably start trending, here are a few of my favourites that will probably be around for a while.

Grey Hair Don't Care

Embrace it or Continue Using Mascara As Cover-Up

I don't care how much grey hair shows up on my noggin—I'm not about to start spraying the areas that need touching up like men in the early '90s were doing with GLH* on their bald spots. Remember those 3 a.m. infomercials? Clearly, whoever decided hair salons are not an essential service doesn't have a vagina. Since I'd be banned for life by my hairdresser if she ever found out I'd purchased boxed dye from a drugstore (although that sample size tube of deep conditioner included in every box is ten times better than any high-end product I've ever tried), for now I accept that little tuft of grey sprouting from the top of my head. At least it hasn't taken over everywhere like most of my friends are experiencing. I choose to believe everyone who's telling me it's cute. But truth be told—I think I'm about to cave though. Very soon I'll be forced to take matters into my own hands, ruining a few white towels and a bathroom mat, and accidentally dying parts of my skin dark black in the process for just $7.99 (when L'Oréal Paris goes on sale).

---

* GLH - Great Looking Hair Product - Life-like fibers men sprayed over their bald spot. A purchase most likely made at 3 a.m. from an infomercial.

Alcoholics Un-Anonymous
Your Get Out of Jail Free Card

The time is now, people! Sadly, I've had more to drink over the past year than ever before. To every ex (alcoholic) boyfriend out there: My SINCEREST THANKS—you taught me well and prepared me for this new world crisis. The student has definitely become the master. I know I'm not the only one whose alcohol consumption has increased along with their waistline. I've got a girlfriend who enjoys a stiff vodka martini on ice every day (without fail) at 4:30 p.m. when *The Young and the Restless* comes on. Own it. It's sort of exciting to think that drinking solo is no longer frowned upon the way it used to be, nor does it make your family worry that perhaps you have a problem that requires intervention. Thanks to COVID it's now totally acceptable to set up a video call with a few gal pals and let the good times flow, or (now that I'm single again) meet a guy virtually for a glass of vino. Yay me!

Also Applies to: COUCHoholics, TALKoholics, HANDWASHING-oholics SANITIZEoholics, WORKOUToholics, BAKEoholics and more!

Karen Memes
Please Stop Throwing Shade

This is just a case of having the wrong name at the wrong time. It seems that the Karen meme was born, or at least given new life, during COVID. And although I've been known to occasionally speak to a manager (#sorrynotsorry) and complain about a thing or two (see chapter: Don't Worry, I'm Not That Karen), I've now turned into the girl who always apologizes for my cursed name whenever

I contact any kind of customer support, prefacing my phone calls or emails or even bot chats (yes I'm fully aware that I'm not talking to a real person) with an "I'm not really a Karen" statement, and/or making sure to act extra nice to compensate for what my parents labelled me at birth.

P*ssy Struggles
The 1970s Called. They Want Their Bush Back

Is it time to move our razors down south (mine hasn't had that honour in years), or allow the au naturel look to make a comeback? You'd think with all the at-home haircuts posted on social media these days that self-grooming would be a no-brainer. But do-it-yourself waxing is messy and sticky, and the reality is that a real man wants a (Sexypringle) woman and not a little girl. Did my latest conquest care even a little bit that the shag carpet did in fact match the curtains? What do you think? Although trust me, it ain't pretty. But it IS liberating! So let's keep this Miranda Hobbes full-blown bush trend going for a little while longer—at least until popping a Tylenol and letting a stranger work on our vajayjays (or going to the girl who's secretly working out of her one-bedroom apartment now) becomes the norm again.

Resting Bitch Face
He Can Actually Tell When I'm Mad Now

Stereotypically, women don't hide their emotions very well. Why should we?! For years, though, we've been able to sculpt our faces and conceal/fake our expressions with the help of a certain botulism and some filler. Thanks to COVID lockdown, though, my Botox girl is no longer on speed dial, and the Zooey Deschanel bangs I've been rocking my whole life are back in style and being put to good use covering up those deeper forehead lines. Bonus? It's no longer a sign of "crazy" to sport a fringe. But man, I'm starting to look like my (real) age of . . . 35? So, it might be time to find one of those underground unlicensed Botox parties I used to attend when they were circulating around Toronto way back in the day and take my chances at not getting botched. That, or accept that the world will now get to see what *surprised* or *confused* looks like on me.

The COVID-19 (AKA The FRESHMAN-15)
Statistically Speaking, I'm Gonna Get Fat

The bread-baking tutorials on my Instagram feed have been blocked since COVID lockdown started (not interested in the carbs). Yet I'm secretly loving the *Chefy Tips* and quarantine cooking lessons from Chef Bruce Bromberg on Instagram, the *Creative Cooking During Corona* Facebook group I joined early on, and all the TikTok trends: feta cheese and cherry tomato pasta, melting cheddar cheese in a waffle maker, and the quesadilla-folding tricks. Need suggestions on how to steer clear of those inevitable COVID-19 pounds of schmaltz? Break up with your boyfriend (heartbreak ruins the appetite which helps with weight loss), or start saying no to grocery store lineups and cut some calories.

Drive-By Birthdays
Could Have Used A Mask Back in the Day

Who knew that regularly driving by my ex-boyfriend's house in an unmarked car, or circling around his block listening to Fiona Apple on repeat when I was younger, was just preparing me for our current world situation? Or that learning how to sneak into his apartment building without ever having to touch a dirty buzzer (there are other ways of getting inside, you know) would help me stay virus-free years later? I'm guessing that Audrey Hepburn scarf I wore back then to hide my identity would be considered an amateur move today. Thanks to COVID, drive-bys (and hiding who we are with masks) are now perfectly acceptable, trending big time actually, and no longer grounds for a restraining order!

Divorce Surges
Oh, It's Coming (Obviously)

Divorce attorneys are already getting an increased number of inquiries, and what's to blame? The Coronavirus quarantine, natch. And although there's little concrete research to suggest that spending too much time together leads to higher divorce rates or break-ups, I've got friends convinced that their partner's remains will end up in their freezer! A new season of *Dexter* is coming out soon I hear, so let's take note. Although, there's only enough room in there for Grey Goose! The romantic in me is hopeful that this trend is not going to stick. Because I truly believe that difficult or trying times should keep us together and motivate us to work harder, rather than tear us apart. I guess we wait on this one, and see how it all plays out. At least a higher divorce rate means more eligible bachelors, right?

Sloppy Seconds
Hoodies & Top Knots Are Here to Stay . . .

Sweatpants have gone from a sign of defeat to basically the only thing my washing machine, or anyone else for that matter, ever sees. So what gives? Well, my waistline, for one. So thank you, COVID, for allowing sweats to become so relevant, and for making that bun also commonly known as the top knot (held up with an '80s scrunchy of course—another comeback!) totally acceptable in public. And as many of us are now finding new ways and reasons to work from home, there is less reason to actually dress up. If you are venturing outside and meeting men or women in real life, "The New Rulebook for First Dates: Sweatpants, No Makeup," is the way to go; the *Wall Street Journal* just confirmed it. This new fashion trend, for every sweatsuit enthusiast out there, has definitely got some staying power, and it's one I'm happy to jump on.

Online Poker
Your Best Bet At "Cashing In" During Lockdown

This is something I really want to join. And no, I'm not bluffing. Because there's actually a lot of money to be made if you know how to play, which I don't. If you've burned through every possible Netflix Original, which we all have by now, it passes the time for those with hours to kill, which again is something we all have at the moment. Plus, it keeps you on a comfy couch (preferably one from Restoration Hardware). And who doesn't love hearing those annoying time clock beeps every two minutes when you're distracting your boyfriend and delaying his hand? Leave him alone; there's plenty of time for other fun activities later on, where the odds are always in your favour.

The COVID Booty Call
Lower the Bar & Reach For Your Phone Instead

Every guy friend I know is currently fucking an old friend right now because no respectable woman is going out and meeting anyone new during COVID. Premium Pussy just isn't an option, so bottom of the barrel will have to do. . . for now. Plus, it's super easy. All you have to do is scroll through your contacts in your phone, find the slut you've been friends with for years and voila, the perfect sitch for someone like you with nothing else going on has fallen straight into your lap. She's easy, available, and reckless. She's The Rebound Girl. The Sloppy Second's Girl. The NSA Girl* who's always DTF. She requires little effort and no work. Hey, don't get me wrong, in the past I too have been this girl, but I'm working hard now to be more of a Bae than a side-chic; a Queen actually. So go ahead boys and indulge. You're in a judge-free zone at the moment. And there's no time like the present. So take advantage of everything you've already got . . . in your phone that is. And P.S. Don't worry about rejection. No one's got standards these days, and they always reply back!

The Guilt-Free Loser
No Need to Lie Anymore to Lock Down a Good Woman

Respect to all the men (and women) out there who had nothing going on before COVID. This is your time to shine and finally be yourself, while collecting CERB,† without judgment. Oh wait, you actually needed to be employed to qualify for this! Lucky for you, you don't have to hide your lifestyle from anyone anymore, let alone lie about having a job on a first date when you don't. Because today, it's perfectly acceptable for a 30-, 40-, or 50-year-old man (or woman) to sit on his (or her) broke ass all day, doing absolutely nothing. It's

. . . .

* NSA -No Strings Attached.

† CERB—Canada Emergency Response Benefit.

actually encouraged and enforced. COVID has given you a FREE PASS, so take it. Your psychiatrist will joke and applaud you during your next online session, commenting on just how ahead of the game you actually are, in comparison to everyone else. You'll be called the real "King (or Queen) of the Couch," and you'll immediately call your friends up to brag about it, feeling uber proud. You do realize your shrink was mocking you (virtually), right? But now your life can remain exactly the same as it's always been, without any adjustments. No more hiding who you really are from anyone, especially a potential new girlfriend or boyfriend or romp. So enjoy this time, or more accurately, the next couple of years off. Relax. Breathe. You now have the perfect excuse to continue doing exactly what you've always done—nothing. You've got this! You're a PRO.

Amazon Sales Are Through the Roof
Help Me, I'm Poor

Although online shopping is a luxury not everyone can afford these days, COVID is making it easy for things to get out of control. So far, I've spent hundreds of dollars on Sephora makeup when I literally haven't worn a stitch of it in over a year, leggings from Aritzia that I wear daily, and every TikTok trend I've come across that involves ordering something (mini waffle maker, rapid egg cooker, LED strip lights, magic butt-lifting yoga pants . . .). But it doesn't end there; Uber Eats is also making a killing off me because I'm simply too lazy to cook now. And my son, who's glued to me 24/7 (except when his public school opens for a month and then immediately shuts back down), manipulates me into buying him Roblox Adopt Me! pets daily just so I can get a half-hour of peace and quiet. He's a genius. But it's a vicious cycle that's guaranteed to send me to the poor house if

I don't watch myself, even though I admit that receiving a package delivery on my front porch, or hearing my doorbell chime, always makes my day. Clearly it doesn't take much anymore. All I can do now is wait for Nordstrom Rack to re-open, and for normal life to re-sume. In the meantime, I guess it's online shopping, Sephora deliveries I won't bother opening, packages galore, and Uber Eats for me.

Conclusion

An Open Letter to Me and My Ex

. . . .

Dear Karen and [insert EX]HAUSTING Struggle,

My nights of sleeping with a smidge of Dentyne Polar Ice in my mouth, stressing the fuck out about my incessant snoring and open mouth breathing caused by the six rhinoplasties I had between the ages of 16 and 25, or waking up at 5 a.m. to sneak out of bed ninja-style so I can re-apply my make-up and pretend I simply wake up looking this damn fabulous every morning, are over. This is me. Morning breath and all. On the plus side, I'm always up, or down (depending on what you're into) for morning sex! So ghost away if I'm not what you're looking for. I promise I'll do the same.

The past few years have been, let's just say . . . cautionary yet entertaining, to say the least. But I'm not broken. I'm not even beaten down. I'm injured, sure, but aren't we all? The thing with most injuries, though, is that they heal. Some heal quickly while others take some time, but they do mend. And my injuries are no different. I've met, dated and fallen in love with some questionable men in my life (noted) which has inevitably led to some bad relationships. Cue the violins. I guess you could say I'm a work in progress: the typical girl who's wasted her time chasing bad boys and losers her whole damn life. But that was then, and this is now. My younger self felt unlovable and highly protective of my damaged heart. Today I feel deserving of love, and excited about future healthy relationships that I know will help heal whatever damage still remains. Yes, I'm a walking cliché. Have been for decades. Shall we add cougar to this stereotypical list too? I'm now in my 40s and nowhere close to where I imagined I'd be at this age. I've never once been married, or engaged, or even shared a mailing address or split the rent with a man (unless we count the five guys I roomed with when I moved into a downtown frat house in my early 20s). What I do have, though, is a beautiful family that I created on my own terms, and I wouldn't change it for the world. Having said all that, I'd be lying if I said there wasn't still something missing.

When my friend Mitch set me up with a very wealthy older gentleman (I'm using this term lightly) a few months back, and this *gentleman* told me on our first date (otherwise known as his audition for my vagina) that he owned two properties, a large house in the 'burbs, and a downtown bachelor pad to take women back to so he never had to reveal his real home address, I recognized the red flag immediately and decided that he wasn't for me. The old Karen might have explored this opportunity, or at least justified it as a lucrative Mr. Right Now while searching for Mr. Right. See, there's been *some* growth! Thanks to every cautionary fail that I've experienced, many of which I've included in this book, I now know exactly who and what I want. But more importantly, I know what I'm not willing to put up with.

Today, if a man doesn't say *bless you* or *gesundheit* when I sneeze, I'm out. If a man doesn't own a Tassimo, which is the true sign of a sociopath, I grab my own morning pick-me-up and send him on his way. Not before parting with a few Mickey D's free coffee stickers that I conveniently keep on the back of my iPhone case of course! And for all those times I remained silent, buried my feelings, pushed my needs aside, or blamed Aunt Flo so you wouldn't think I was over-reacting, desperate, or being too needy? I should have shared whatever I was feeling without the fear of critique or abandonment. To all the women out there who are still single . . . we need to stop second-guessing ourselves! I didn't recognize this before, but I do now. I'm starting to know and appreciate my own self-worth. My days of wanting to fix, change, or wait around for broken men with inflated egos to get their shit together are over. Please do not call or text again . . . "new phone, who dis?"

My time for real true love will come. I'm hopeful and optimistic. Today I notice things; like really truly notice. Not only to what you say, but also when your actions lack consistency. I now make a mental note of everything, rather than just ignoring things like I used to do in the past. Here's the thing—the universe delivers the warning signs, and our gut then confirms everything. In the end, it's up to us to decide what to do with all this insight. Finally, I'm WOKE. Please exit to your left.

Good, healthy, stable men who want real, monogamous, lasting relationships based on trust, loyalty, love, friendship and equal partnership are out there and trending. GoFundMe. It's time to give one of these guys a chance and ditch the (*Squid*) games for good. Lost souls are so 2019. So the struggle continues . . .

I will find my version of Mr. McDreamy, flip my narrative and then my hair . . . and finally get my happy ending. This I know. It's a done deal. Except my HAPPY ENDING, unlike the one my ex-boyfriend will never admit to receiving, won't be taking place in Sin City or on a dirty massage table!

STILL WANNA DATE ME?

All Future Dates, Boyfriends, Husbands, Flings, DILFs (Dads I'd Like To Fuck), Chubby Chasers (yes, I've gained a few COVID pounds), Booty Calls, Situationships, Rhinos (Male Cougars), Side-Pieces, Sugar Daddies, or New BFFs (no one replaces JoJo, obvs), please flip page, date, and sign.

The Non Disclosure Agreement has been drafted for your protection (and mine). So read it carefully. Yes, getting involved with a writer can be messy. If things don't work out, instead of stabbing you with a ball-point pen (FYI, fountain pens are way sharper), we take every experience we've ever had with you, and all those horrible impressions you left on us, and pen that shit to paper. But it's a moot point moving forward thanks to all my newfound growth. Next time my choices will be better. My relationships will be better. Most importantly, I will be better. I promise. Just in case, let's put our Johnny Hancocks in writing first, knowing that WHAT-EVER happens, it'll stay strictly between us.

Non Disclosure Agreement

PARTIES

- This Non Disclosure Agreement (hereinafter referred to as the "Agreement") is entered into on _____ (The "Effective Date"), by and between _____, with an address of _____ (hereinafter referred to as the "Disclosing Party" and _____ with an address of _____ (hereinafter the "Receiving Party")(collectively referred to as the "Parties").

CONFIDENTIAL INFORMATION

- All parties agree to keep personal information, mishaps, what happened behind closed doors, or in the bedroom, no matter how nasty, completely confidential. Meaning, I won't write a SEQUEL about you if things don't work out between us. Your Privacy Will Be Protected.

- Confidential information refers to any data and/or information that is related to the Disclosing Party and in any form including, but not limited to, oral or written. Such confidential information is, but not limited to, any information related to the Relationship of the Disclosing Party, Receiving Party and more.

- Receiving Parties include, but are not limited to, Future Boyfriend(s), Future Husband(s), and/or Future Other(s).

RETURN OF CONFIDENTIAL INFORMATION

- The Receiving Party agrees not to disclose, copy, clone, modify, any confidential information related to the Disclosing Party and in any form, including but, not limited to, oral or written. Such confidential information is, but not limited to, any information related to the Relationship between the Disclosing Party and the Receiving Party.

OWNERSHIP
- This Agreement is non transferable and may only be transferred by a written consent provided by both parties.

TIME PERIODS
- The Non Disclosure provisions of this Agreement shall survive the termination of this Agreement and Receiving Party's duty to hold Confidential Information in confidence shall remain in effect until the Confidential Information no longer qualifies as a trade secret or until Disclosing sends Receiving Party written notice releasing Receiving Party from this Agreement, whichever comes first. Copyright © 2021 NonDisclosureAgreement.com. All Rights Reserved.

WAIVER
- The failure to exercise any right provided in this Agreement shall not be a waiver of prior or subsequent rights.

EXIT CLAUSE
- If things work out and both parties get their HAPPY ENDING, Disclosing Party and Receiving Party are free to rip up this Legal Agreement and tell the world about the relationship. Scream about it from the roof tops or incessantly post on social media, every last G-ddamn detail without any legal ramifications.

SEVERABILITY

- If a court finds any provisions of this Agreement invalid or unenforce-
  able, the remainder of this Agreement shall be interpreted so as best
  to affect the intent of the parties.

GOVERNING LAW

- This Agreement shall be governed by and construed in accordance
  with the laws of _____.

SIGNATURE AND DATE

- The Parties hereby agree to the terms and conditions set forth in this
  Agreement and such is demonstrated throughout their signatures below.

DISCLOSING PARTY   **RECEIVING PARTY**

_____   _____

DATE: _____   **DATE:** _____

Acknowledgments

Thankfully, most of the people I offend in this book don't read. Or they have blocked me on social media and will never find out. To those that do and wonder if I feel bad about all the things I've said? I don't. Well, maybe just a little . . . but not enough to keep me up at night. Honestly, I have the best Ambien sleeps.

To everyone who has inspired me and held my hand throughout this entire process—thank you. You know who you are.

A big shout-out to Harlow Books for taking a chance on a new writer who essentially was just trying to get over yet another break-up. To my editor Lisa Balaban, I'm beyond grateful for your wisdom, advice, and all the hours you spent perfecting my manuscript. Without your help, this would have ended up being just a sad, handwritten diary. Amanda Storey, thanks for your proofreading skills. To my brilliant Professor Uncle, three cheers (or scoops of hummus as per your payment request) for all the free advice. To Katrina Ciccone-Piccole, I still owe you a martini for helping me out early on. Lewelin Polanco, thank you for turning my manuscript into a real book. Your layout suggestions and design treatment throughout was on point—plus, you were so much fun to work with! To my lawyer, thanks for reassuring me that "it isn't defamation if it's all FUCKING true."

To all my friends, some mentioned, others not, you gave me the strength to put it all out there. I love you all for standing by me during every (bad) relationship, and for picking up the phone (and the pieces) after things were done. Donnie, you are always right. To Jojo Pearl, you are the true definition of what friendship is. Mitch Wolfe, thanks for mentoring me. To Joey (AKA, Von) McGuirk, all the contributions you made and the hours we spent on my balcony getting tipsy and laughing about every ridiculous ex, was invaluable. George Stroumboulopoulos, thank you for agreeing to write the foreword for this book. If you wanna give things another go, feel free to sign the enclosed Non Disclosure Agreement so we can get this party started—again. For those who can't tell when I'm making a joke . . . well that's on you.

To past boyfriends and terrible dates, who provided me with endless material and more than enough lessons learned—sayonara. Get your own publishing deal if you want to challenge any of my truths, memories or misadventures. Or, just do better the next time around—with the next girl.

And lastly, thank you to my wonderful son who sat alongside me every day during COVID while I wrote this. Just like that emotional support puppy we all want but don't qualify for, you too waited patiently for a treat—and of course an ending. You've been my biggest cheerleader all along, as I am yours. Always and forever. Xo